Puri-
FIRE

Puri-FIRE:

USING THE STORMS OF LIFE TO
IGNITE YOUR LIFE'S PURPOSE

WRITTEN BY DR. JOHN L. MASON

Puri-FIRE: Using the Storms of Life to Ignite Your Life's Purpose
By Dr. John L. Mason

Copyright © 2018 Dr. John L. Mason
All rights reserved

Billion Soul Publishing
PO Box 623307
Oviedo, Florida 32762
(407) 563-4806
www.billionsoulpub.com

ISBN 13: 978-0-9989773-7-9
ISBN 10: 0998977373

First Edition
14 15 16 17 18 —1 12 11 10 9 8 7 6
Printed in the United States of America

DEDICATION

This work is dedicated to many individuals and organizations, that without their collective tireless efforts this work would be for naught.

Arlena Mason - Mommy, though you will have to read the "celestial" version, you know what you have done.

The original Dr. John L. Mason (Sr.) - Yours is the reality that no matter how I may choose to argue with your influence, the results are clearly in this work.

Nanny Goat - I pray you see yourself in these pages. I don't call like I should, but allow this apology to echo around the world; I'm sorry.

To my extended family: Linda, K-Mac, Nik, Kia, Santy, Tooty, and the Dominator - Don't you ever sell your dreams short, give them to someone else because they are too large, or stop because the weight is too great. To whom much is given, much is required.

Dr. Belinda Brownlee & The New Holly Light Baptist Church College and Career Class - Thank you for putting the original book in my hand over 20 years ago. I now give back to you my life's work.

Pastor Calvin and Kimberly Tibbs & The Kingdom Dominion Church Family - My spiritual covering, and role models, words cannot tell you what your *"Love Led Encounters"* have meant.

Legacy, purpose, calling, gifts, and daily influence are more than words to you.

Dr. Patricia Whitelocke & The Bibleway Family - We have been taught for nearly 50 years to "get all we can and can all we get". For such a time as this were we put into this world.

Dr. James E. Victor, Jr. - Son, a better friend NO MAN could ask for. A greater influence NO MAN could ever ask for. A more amazing demonstration of God's goodness NO MAN could ever ask for.

Fonda Austin - Quietly you have motivated me. Steadfastly you have supported each leg of this project. Now, rejoice WITH me!

And Finally, Shamin Y. Mason (Baby Girl) - What can I say to a young lady who has proven through demonstration that she listens, absorbs, and walks out her father's instructions. You have proven that Ephesians 6:1-3 is REAL:

> Children, obey your parents in the Lord [that is, accept their guidance and discipline as His representatives], for this is right [for obedience teaches wisdom and self-discipline]. 2 Honor [esteem, value as precious] your father and your MOTHER [and be respectful to them]—this is the first commandment with a promise— 3 so that it may be well with you, and that you may have a long life on the earth.

To those I have not named, but you know who you are... Thank you!

FOREWORD

"It takes one to know one," is a phrase often heard by opponents who find themselves at odds with one another. "Name calling" is at the heart of this manner of verbal teasing; and names are important, since we govern our lives around them. But *Puri–FIRE* is not name calling, it's flame throwing!

It makes sense that a person shaped by fire should in turn write about fire. There is no wonder that John Mason, a professional educator, impactful church leader and business consultant, would be chosen by God to recount his over two decades of a flame-formed life. Fireworks! Fire hurts, and especially so when the soul of a person is the target of a fire's fury.

Within this writing though, readers will be inspired by the sparks of commonality they encounter, and set ablaze by transformative truths that connect Dr. Mason's personal accounts with ready-to-use ways to ignite change. You may find yourself reflecting in the flames of your own thoughts, as each chapter takes you to places of pure consciousness where God revisits ideas He previously placed within your own experience.

Prepare to stoke the flames of your own heart by contemplating what people will remember about you, what your life produced, and how individuals are currently being affected by your body of work. Well before you have completed the last chapter, John Mason will have introduced you to the flames God still uses to refine people He loves, and since you have selected this tool to cultivate your moments, enjoy the purity of the fire as the hidden gems of your spiritual DNA emerge from the pages of *Puri-FIRE*.

Dr. J. Calvin Tibbs, Pastor
Kingdom Dominion Church

TEST 0

I failed. Not only did I fail, but I miserably failed every test. I thought I was equipped to handle the issues facing me: relationships, health, aging, church, friendships, gossip, trustworthiness, ethics, promises, fidelity, but I failed. Everywhere. It was not that I did not know the trials were coming. It was not that I did not speak with others about the severity of the trials, or that I did not prepare. What I did not do, however, was look at the very foundation of my being. I did not dig deeply enough to uncover what made me "tick." The pillars of my character remained untouched, unobserved, and unfortunately compromised. My failures, sadly enough, were avoidable.

I bought a book titled *Twelve Tests of Character*[1] by Harry Emerson Fosdick at a roadside shop in Central, South Carolina over twenty-five years ago. It had long been out of print even then, but the title intrigued me. I was amused by the language, images, and standards mirrored in the book from that time period. It amazed me that life had changed so drastically, and that our values were so removed from Fosdick's account. I brought this up to my college and career Sunday school class of the New Holly Light Baptist Church. They pointed out a simple, but startling, revelation: Fosdick's fiery character tests were still relevant today. It was only the vehicle for delivering them that was outdated. They encouraged me to translate the essence of the book into the language and substance of today's society. It was necessary, they believed, to prepare people to face the challenges that life would bring their way. It has literally taken me twenty-three years, three states, four

---

[1] Harry Emerson Fosdick, *Twelve Tests of Character*, New York: Harper & Row, 1923.

church transitions, and my fiftieth birthday to rework Fosdick's timeless classic for today, but here it is.

TABLE OF CONTENTS

THE INTRODUCTION TO THE TESTS

Almost a century has passed since Fosdick's *Twelve Tests of Character* were written. To say the least, much has changed. Character is now regarded as a changeable position, free to adapt to a person's circumstances. Gone are the absolutes and standards that were foundational to the development of a person's character. Fosdick made it clear that a man or woman's character must transcend the storms and challenges of life. This is only possible if their character was built upon standards that could withstand those storms in the first place. Our nation's structure and belief system is changing daily. Our cities find themselves in a constant state of unrest as poverty and its many problems assault them. Our families are fighting to survive due to a skyrocketing divorce rate in a culture that is not designed to keep them together. Individuals find themselves seeking ways to illuminate their personal search for meaning and purpose as quickly as possible. Is it at all surprising that character is no longer a prerequisite for being a mature and productive citizen? Only a people who are firmly rooted in the truth of Scripture understand how character shapes the world we live in. Its development has the power to ensure the health of our nation. Integrity matters. So does honesty and purity. Character isn't a perk; it's vital.

In 1923 Harry Emerson Fosdick quoted the Chinese proverb, "You cannot carve rotten wood." He provided a clear explanation: "Nor can you make impressions upon a decrepit and decayed character. The development of character is an old point of emphasis, but it is indispensable, and maybe now we may well get back to it." Fosdick was ahead of his time in understanding that the very strength and resiliency of our country were dependent on the development of the inner character of our citizens. Fosdick understood that character served as the rails upon which each person's engine would carry their life's train toward an ultimate end. The smallest defect in the track could derail the entire line of cars. We see this unhappy picture playing itself out in the world today as leaders fall because of a lack of integrity. The twelve tests of Fosdick's book reminded the reader that there were basic standards for living that "our new generation is tempted to forget."

Character is more than "who you are when no one is looking." Character is the DNA that you leave behind when you interact with anyone at any time. And those interactions are important! The wide variety of these interactions account for the many reactions others have to us. We are: generous, rude, hotheaded, shy, giving, loving, patient, boring, talkative, aloof, good listeners, self-centered, a piece of work, arrogant, unreachable, spoiled, condescending, incompetent, precious, or simply amazing, according to how we choose to treat others. There seems to be no rhyme or reason behind why someone acts one way or another in relationship to someone else, but our actions have a ripple effect to those around us. Unfortunately, Fosdick asserts that we no longer want to be defined by standards and principles that may prove to be the antithesis of present-day trends. In other words, we do not wish to be identified with any action that is counterculture or unpopular. We do not want to be obedient to any absolutes. What should our position be? Should we develop a mindset that allows us to be known for what we "believe" or is it better to be known for what we can accomplish?

"By any means necessary" has become the mantra of our society. Just get it done! It doesn't matter how! These words are echoed in boardrooms, classrooms, meetings, and discussions as we attempt to complete the tasks before us. Few organizations maintain processes in which the product only moves forward if it meets the rigors for the agreed-upon standards of the company. This level of quality control insures that the DNA of the product conveys a simple, aligned set of messages to the consumer. *This is the level of consistency we desire.* Unfortunately, we are not willing to put in the time to yield ourselves to these greater standards and principles all the time. The result is a Frankenstein-like character that is a mixture of standards, hustles, tricks, short cuts, camouflage, justifications, and compromises. Character produced like this will not pass Fosdick's fiery tests.

I was taught as a child that if you wanted to know the true nature of a thing, you should set it on fire. Much to the consternation of my mother, I did this on a regular basis. You can only imagine the dismay on her face, as the grill became my quality-testing laboratory. Everything was set ablaze in hopes of finding out what it was composed of. Most of the time, I found that fire only dissolved the item into a puddle of indiscernible goo. (Sorry, Nannette! Your Barbie dolls were sacrificed for the greater good of science.) Yet, for other items, the fire burned away surface byproducts, leaving a pure substance. If you burn wood, you end up with pure charcoal in the end. This same principle, I found out, is used in industry for the training of leaders. Place a person in a difficult position, and you will see how the heat of the moment shines light on the pillars of their character. For example, a person who works for a college or university may find him or herself given the task of increasing the savings of the institution. Their solution? Authorize the use of substandard materials, supplies, and products instead of the ones being used presently. This solution is directed toward tricking the bottom-line savings, but it does not reflect real leadership skills or innovative ideas on the part of the one given that task. Why was this solution even considered? Because the leader was guided by his own underdeveloped inner standards without consideration of the quality the college was pledged to maintain. This could only end in conflict with the college. This is only one example of how character affects decision-making.

These pages extract truths and information from Fosdick's 1923 book, hundreds of leadership development texts, countless hours of paternal life lessons, and the timeless wisdom of the Bible's character development plan. Do not be fooled, however; these pages are not written for those who are eager to make changes in their lives. These lessons are written for: those who have no faith in humanity, those who see no good in role models, those who cannot find the oft-ignored path, those who have been burned countless times, those labeled the black sheep of their families, those who were given a test of moral character and failed miserably, those who have been told by others around them that they are worthless, those who are in complete and total denial, and those who have given up on life and change altogether. These aforementioned people are disillusioned, dismayed, down, and in their minds, defeated. This book is intended to assist these disillusioned warriors to attain something better, by becoming something better. To this group of future overcomers, I have poured out my heart.

TEST 1

PUTTING FIRST THINGS FIRST:
THE ENEMY OF FOCUS IS MULTITASKING

"**Sorry I couldn't** get to the phone. I was on a video conference while watching Timmy's Little League game, and catching up with my neighbor!" Sound familiar? Our current society knows little of singleness of mind. If it were possible we would handle as many things on our to-do list as possible at the very same time! While this sounds like a great idea, the reality is that the more balls we put into play, the more poorly we execute *all the tasks*. So what if Johnny can't read? Does it really matter that a car only lasts three years? I really look forward to repeating myself since you were not paying attention! Really? Most folks I know are fed up with being part of a "to-do" list. Our preoccupation with "stuff" is deeply rooted in the first area that will be tested in your life: Do you make time for the things that will permanently and indelibly change your life, or is change a casualty of the raging war over what preoccupies you right now?

Establishing What Matters

We are often a confused and preoccupied people. We say we know what is most important to us, but our values have become more and more situationally based: Under this set of circumstances *this* is important, but under a different set *that* is important. No wonder our current society has been called wishy-washy and direction-less by those older than we are. The children of the twenty-first century, Millennials and Generation Z, often struggle with con-structing solid and unchanging pillars in their lives. They were not birthed into a world where absolutes were cherished as most important. The importance of concepts such as God, love, patience, authority, family, community, a work ethic, education, universal acceptance, stability, and basic values themselves have become subject to debate. They are consid-ered vital or not, depending on the audience. Overall, these concepts have lost their luster for the younger generations. I don't think we started out planning to diminish their impor-tance. We just allowed other things to get in their way. Our pre-occupation was seen, unfortunately, as a statement of priority. We did the things that we deemed important, and ignored those things that were not. So what if we didn't go to church this week? So what if we didn't feel like having company at our house this year? The less fortunate aren't my responsibility, are they? I have my life goals accomplished; it is up to you to take care of yours, right? Why do you think that I owe any-thing to "them" just because I live here? The twenty-first cen-tury has manifest a clear picture of a world that is increasingly filled with the importance of materialism (for me), selfishness (me), isolationism (just me), elitism (because of me), being enti-tled (you owe me), and disrespecting authority (you talking to me?). There's also open condemnation of difference/open condemnation of those who do not accept difference, and other changes: The church is seen as obsolete; the family as a structure is no longer desirable; marriage is now a temporary union based on changing criteria; and there is no longer a solid blueprint for success. Under these conditions, putting first things first becomes a *huge* undertaking. It is not, however, impossible. The first step is your desire to want to establish priorities. This may not happen until your world is spiraling so out of control that you must make a change. This may not happen until you have hit the bottom of that spiral. Or you may just be sick and tired of being sick and tired. Take a deep breath, and get ready for some good news!

Assessing Where You Are

Now that you have decided to do something different, please take a few minutes and determine where you are. No, not the rose-colored glasses version, but

the real, nasty, unfiltered, un-Photoshopped version. The "I cannot provide for my family" version. The "I have not had a job since I cut grass as a twelve-year-old" version. The "I cannot even dream of owning a house" version. The "I am tired of crying myself to sleep" version. If you are not honest with yourself, you cannot make an honest assessment. The brutal part of putting first things first is determining what should be first, and what imposter is currently in its place. This step may take the longest, but it is well worth the time. Ask yourself five core questions:

1. What is the most important thing in my life?
2. What makes me happy all the time?
3. What am I striving to become?
4. If money was not an issue, what would I do? Become?
5. What factors are holding me back?

To do this, get out a notebook and put them on paper. Sit down and take your time. It may even be wise to do it over a period of days, so you can get down to the nitty-gritty. By answering these questions honestly, you will begin the process of identifying your core values. The next step is to take them and determine what you are going to be known for once you are no longer here.

Setting Up a Plan

I have challenged, and have been challenged by many of my students, to keep a journal of how time is spent. This simple activity gives

a clear picture of what a person does with the 86,400 seconds appointed to each day. The inglorious outcome of the time mirror, however, is that we cannot seem to justify choices that have no eternal value or lasting qualities. What kinds of choices fit here? Hmm. Let's see…Facebook, YouTube, Skype, Snapchat, Instagram, Pinterest, Twitter, Periscope, endless Internet surfing, phone calls, movies, and a billion computer games. This is not to say that these cannot be used for good, but the vast majority of activities completed through these media have no lasting value. These diversions are designed to help the common person relax, unwind, decompress, and manage their lives. But do they really do that? A person cannot regain a single second wasted on this stuff! They are gone forever! Any possible positive use of this time is also gone. That conversation with a struggling high school student that would result in their rededication to their studies—Gone! The reassurance of the single mother that she was not alone, that others had been in the same position, but came through— Gone! Getting around to that book that your pastor suggested that you read—Gone! Having time with your children—Gone! Taking care of your health—Gone! Studying the Word of God—Gone! Having more than shallow relationships with people—Gone!

Most changes begin with a truthful, transparent, and ongoing assessment of your difficulty with setting priorities.

We miss 100 percent of the things we do not focus on accomplishing. We will also mismanage 100 percent of the priorities we do not assign! Here's the question to ask people: "What is going to take most of your attention today?" Many will tell you they don't know. Instead of following a goal, they will wait for whatever *requires* attention, and do that. Yes, the squeaky wheel syndrome is alive and well! The squeaky wheel, however, rarely makes a huge difference in our lives. *Substantial change requires not only a plan, but also a system.*

Work Your Plan

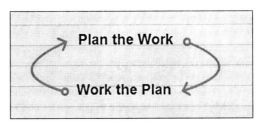

Ironically, the greatest enemy of a plan is your inability to *stick* to it! Without daily commitment and consistency, a person will allow himself to be taken from his well-designed course.

There are those who have the whole "mind-over-matter" thing down to a science. They think a thing, they map a thing, they execute the thing, and they attain their goal. For them this process is their law. It does not move, it does not bend, it does not change, and thus, it is the standard for their life. Unfortunately, they think that *everyone* in the world will have the same level of success if they use the same steps. They also think everyone should be like them! Well, we won't and we don't want to be! Society is only now accepting that what works for one may not definitely work for another if they do the same thing. Everyone is uniquely different. Every person has a list of things that are like low-hanging fruit for them. They can master these items quickly. In these areas, they can dispense with the enemy with a quickness that makes others shake their heads in amazement. These same people have other types of fruit growing at the tip-top of their trees. Getting to that requires planning, tools, strategy, and often help. Those who were so successful in other matters are now petrified by fear! Their former successes are of no consolation as they procrastinate about even thinking about these out-of-reach issues. Then comes the brutal reality of the advice of friends and family: "Just do it!" they say. And the battle cries come: "You will be successful when you are ready." "The only reason you are stuck here is because you *want* to be."

What a trap! It never entered my mind that my strength may be your weakness, and vice versa. If I do not recognize that I am speaking from an it's-easy-to-handle-this-low-hanging-fruit-of-mine position, I may be damaging you because you cannot reach the same fruit in your life that I can in mine. You have done nothing wrong! We should be thankful for our successes. They can be used as road maps for everyone else, but only when their core components are identified and set up as pillars for others to follow. We cannot blindly pattern ourselves off one another and expect success. We can only apply principles and use blueprints. How they work with each one will be somewhat different according to their unique strengths and weaknesses. Here's a list of what we can do:

- Set a clear picture of where you want to go.
- Take a snapshot of where you are. Be realistic in where you are right now.
- Set attainable, realistic goals that when combined will lead to your larger end success. (Put this on paper!)
- Place a *realistic* timeline on the overall process. Check this with someone else, just in case you are not good at judging the time needed to reach your goal. (We can be in too much of a hurry, expecting too much, too fast.)

- *Measure* each and every step you take: positive and negative.
- Forgive yourself when you miss, and celebrate when you achieve a goal.
- Attach yourself to others on similar journeys for strength, accountability, and help.

We know this process. We function with this process every single day. In fact, we have become so good at it that folks cannot fool us into believing that we have overlooked a step when we have proof to the contrary. The strength of this process is that it must be used for every single situation. We do not have the luxury of omitting a situation because it is not "important enough" to maintain. It is the small issues that over time become the monsters we fight and fear.

One of the most powerful tools regarding time, its use, and its management is to make your appointments accountable for themselves. Curious statement, huh? If your appointments are allowed to run amuck in your life, very soon you will serve them. So ask each and every appointment a straightforward question: "Why are you on my schedule, and what value will you add to my life?" If there is no plausible answer to your question, get rid of that appointment! Be sure to look at every part of your life. Leave nothing out.

Evaluate Your Progress and Correct Your Course (Life's GPS)

There are times when I am driving to an unfamiliar business or home and have to use my GPS. Today's technology makes this almost intuitive: Type in the address, listen to the voice prompts, arrive safely! Almost...There are instances when you follow the directions, but for some reason you don't fully trust them. What happens then? Yep! "Recalculating! Make a safe and legal U-turn when possible." The same holds true when we are putting first things first in our lives. Because we are following the simple process of measuring our successes and failures we know *exactly* where we are in our progress toward the end goal. Again, if we do not make the correction of issues while they are small, we may have a much larger problem on our hands. A classic example of this principle is the time I was visiting a colleague at a campus where I had never been. My GPS was clear, concise, and *wrong!* I followed every instruction given, and I ended up going back and forth down a road looking for an exit off the interstate that did not exist. Using the principle above, I stopped the car, called for new instructions, and changed my route. If you find yourself off course, do not continue down a road in which you have no faith or confidence. Stop, seek intervention from someone who has better answers than you (friends, accountability partners, or the Father above) and change course. You will find that putting first things first is a habit that pays immediate and amazing dividends.

Technobabble

Our current world has made this section necessary, and for that I apologize. It is heartbreaking that we have to lose or break our phones for there to be peace in our lives. We live in a world of multiple devices. This obsession with electronics begins with toddlers, and spirals out of control as we mature. Now we must have shared technological platforms in which our phones, tablets, laptops, desktops, watches, and cars can all talk to one another. What on earth is so important that we need to do this? What earth-shattering crisis requires this level of synchronization? In a word, we have become addicted to access.

Access to "stuff"

This "stuff" is the core of our multiple interests: sports, entertainment, global events, spiritual awakening, self-improvement, social climbing, networking, banking, gossip, and yes, communication. Each and every area of these possible addictions is a threat to the priorities you have set for yourself. *Each and every area of possible addiction must be managed.* It is impossible to maintain an uncluttered priority list if your addictions speak louder than your commitments. Why do I call them "possible addictions"? In this technologically rich age, we must be wary of the influence and grip that these items have on our lives. Fosdick did not have such issues. There was but one telephone. Mail came to a central box located in front of the house. Most conversations were face-to-face. A lazy afternoon was often spent reading a book, listening to live music, or sitting on the porch with family and friends. What a different world that was! The complications of our current society are obstacles of our own construction, and the more we engage with them, the more isolated from others we become. The good news is that they can be removed as easily as they were built.

Putting First Things First

The bottom line of this test is simple: Establish the priority list. Eliminate anything that stands in the way of your main priority, and then measure both the progress toward the goal and the goals themselves. There is no such things as equal priorities. Something will take precedence in your life. Don't let those things that preoccupy you become your priority. Don't let those "squeaky wheels" run the show. Decide on your chief goal. Once we have come to grips with the fact that there is a singular "top priority," we are ready to complete our list. With foundational principles in place, there is no reason for us to allow a level "C" priority to run our lives. In fact, there is no reason to allow a lower-ranking priority to do anything but wait its turn! Instead we can live our lives intentionally, with a focus on reaching that goal. If we do this, we will be successful in putting first things first.

This, like most things we do not wish to do, will take time and practice to master. We often allow ourselves to drift. We drift away from the shores we know so well. This is not a violent or turbulent process; it is a gentle lulling that results in the land growing smaller and smaller in our sight. Drifting is preventable only when we admit that it is a natural occurrence, and it is to be expected. Then, and only then, are we on our guard to:

- Identify it when it happens,
- Take the necessary steps to stay on course, and
- Recalculate our route based on the change in our position.

Without that last step—recalculating—we will waste precious resources in meeting our goals. This may take some folks a bit of time to wrap their minds around. Put these tools in your toolbox and be patient with yourself as you make these changes. Just remember that you will gain confidence in every subject and task that you put your mind to completing. In the meantime, allow the tools of this chapter to become a part of your daily routine and arsenal.

> **"Preoccupation is the most common form of failure" – Harry Fosdick Emerson**

Stoke the Fire

1. Why is it so easy to fall into the multitasking trap? What strategy can you use today to take a strong step forward?

2. Many of you are afraid of making changes in your lives. What is at the core of this fear? What will you do to take control of your life?

3. Priorities are often like monuments—once constructed they last forever. I have found that the priorities I have now are not the same as those I had in other seasons of my life. How have your priorities changed over time? Is it time to change them again?

4. In the corporate world, there is an old saying, "If you don't measure it, it does not matter." Do you have a way to measure all your goals? Which of your priorities are still missing ways to measure them? How many of you are still telling little white lies about your progress?

5. I have read that priorities are not rules, but really good suggestions. If that is true when life gets hard, we are no longer responsible for moving within our priorities. What can you do on a daily basis to validate that you are walking according to your priorities?

Bonus: Have you charted your current course? If not, what are you waiting for? If you are off course, where do you wish to end up?

TEST 2

EARTHQUAKE-PROOF YOUR LIFE: IS YOUR FOUNDATION BIG ENOUGH FOR YOUR STRUCTURE?

The second test of your life rests upon your ability to grow in your life according to the foundation that you have in place. The greater the building under construction, the greater the foundational footprint it  must rest upon. This is a universal truth in both architecture and construction. Prior to the mechanized, modern versions of these sciences, experts in this area relied upon their vast experience to insure building stability. Fosdick used a camping example in 1923. He stated, "Any camper acquainted with tents recognizes the figure. When you pitch a tent, if you lengthen the ropes you must strengthen the stakes." Unfortunately for most modern lives, we have left camping in our youth with scouting programs and backyard getaways. Today we have "instant" tents with no ropes. Stakes go down at the corners for stability though just the same. The principle, however, still stands to the present day: *If you extend the ropes of your life, you must have foundational integrity.*

What Is Your Life Built to Sustain?

God is without question the greatest Architect, Foreman, and Master Builder that will ever exist. The tree is without question His most inspiring example of this principle. Picture the most majestic tree you have ever seen. It is tall, wide, breathtaking, and architecturally perfect. Why? A tree is made by God to naturally follow the laws of building integrity: the more branches and the higher the tree grows, the deeper and wider the roots grow. Every tree will grow in this pattern. Humans are not programmed in this way. Inherent in our DNA is the power of choice. Although we may *think* about the correct ratios for our lives, this is not always sufficient motivation to follow the best courses of action available to us. In other words, even though we see that particular habits are tearing us down, we do not always get rid of them; and even though we see the need to be honest in a situation to build trust, we do not always follow through as we should. Our lives are constructed to either maintain greatness, or topple under the weight of overextension or shoddy character choices. We determine which of these outcomes will be a reality based on the culmination of our habits, experiences, and foundational principles. Your life is built; it does not happen by accident, and it is not a series of coincidences. Any building process requires approved plans, quality building materials, a knowledgeable construction team, and time. Most of us get into trouble with the very first steps! We do not submit our plans for approval; we use whatever materials we can get our hands on; we believe we can do the work ourselves; and we want it done tomorrow. It is no wonder that our buildings crumble at our feet, or are condemned by the authorities when they come under scrutiny. They have not been built according to the approved blueprints of the Master Builder using His materials under the direction of His Holy Spirit and submitted to His schedule. This must change.

What Are Your Foundational Principles?

In the last chapter we talked about putting first things first. This included a deliberate assessment of the "pillars" of your life. This test also resulted in sticking to your priorities once they were established. A quietly kept secret is that your priorities form the frame upon which every single dream, purpose, and pursuit will one day rest. Priorities serve as the "roots" from which your visible projects will soar into the sky. Where there are no established priorities, there will be no branches or fruit in your life's work.

These foundational principles can be well illustrated in the science behind the earthquake-proofing of skyscrapers. Interestingly, the oldest *wooden* structure on Earth is a temple in Japan built in the 700s A.D. It has survived numerous major earthquakes. Scientists have looked at the way this and other pagodas are built to help them in erecting huge buildings in other areas of the world prone to earthquakes. How have these pagodas, some of which are over a thousand years old, maintained their strength? Studies found the remarkable reason these buildings are still standing today. They have hundreds of flexible, interlocking beams that are joined together so that when the earth moves, the building jiggles and gives with the movement in different directions. This prevents it from toppling over.[2] These small beams are hidden from the eye, but indispensable to the longevity of the structure itself. You can't see them, but someone took the time to carefully fit them in there. So it is with us. When devastating trials (our earthquakes) come into our lives, our responses show forth our character. If solid character has been built within us, we have the patience and flexibility to give and remain standing.

How Do You Test the Stages of Construction?

Construction is a very precise science. You cannot just hope for a quality house; you must take steps to insure quality in the end product. Our lives are no different. Without the necessary "inspections" your building may not be up to the right standards. A substandard building may not be condemned, but it will never live up to the expectations of its owner. This fact makes the inspection of your building, through every phase of the building process, remarkably important.

Make Sure Your Foundation Is Firm

The initial step in insuring that you have a quality building is to submit plans that include a foundation that will support your structure. There are no accidental skyscrapers. These impressive buildings are designed to include the minutest details. Very rarely is a novice able to attain the level of detail and precision required for the approval of a building plan. (You can be sure the craftsman who designed those temples were the best of

---

[2] An absolutely fascinating clip on how this works can be found on YouTube at https://www.youtube.com/watch?v=0tFWn_e71qc.

the best too!) When we are children, we bounce back and forth between ideas: We want to be a...fireman, doctor, astronaut, teacher, NFL star, video game designer, engineer, architect, and on goes the list. All of these professions have merit, but may not align with the knowledge, skills, abilities, and gifts within us. Once we have identified what is in us, then we can identify where best to use our gifts and talents. Once we know what our purpose is, we can "buy into it" by allowing those who are older, wiser, more seasoned, or trained access into our lives. Allowing these people to speak into our lives is critical to our development. Self-made men and women are not completely unfamiliar to us, but they are very much like finding a unicorn in someone's backyard! Most people are mentored by others and grow through those relationships. Most people have teachers who train them to accomplish the tasks they have been created to finish.

Invest in Quality Building Materials

This step cannot be overlooked or ignored. You cannot expect to have a quality product using shoddy building materials. This simply will not work. "Cutting corners" or building quickly with substandard building materials will always produce a substandard building. There's an old saying: "You can't make a silk purse out of a pig's ear." Using poor materials instead of the ones approved in your good building plan will have a bad effect in the end. How can you prevent this? Put first things first by investing in quality materials (the right stuff for your growth), the proper processes (the right path for your feet), and trained personnel (the right teachers for your mission). Last of all, put checks and balances in place (the right accountability for your life). And then work carefully: "Measure twice, cut once."

If we treated each project as if we were completing it for a person we held in high esteem, I doubt if any of us would allow poor workmanship. We would protest if the work was not up to the right standard. We would confront anyone who was trying to do things poorly, and we would not rest until things were done correctly. Honor and action are tethered to the heart, purpose, and foundation of a person. What you honor you will act upon, and what you hold as unimportant, you will ignore. We must take action about our own destiny. If we are going to be built in a strong way to "get the job done," we must take responsibility for all these aspects of our growth. We can't just leave them to the whims of fortune. With a blueprint in hand, we can take action accordingly to bring us the satisfaction and success we desire.

Surround Yourself with a Knowledgeable Team

You cannot complete this construction process by yourself. History has proven that the best-laid plans are those that are the result of wise counsel. When a person brings the best minds together to bear on a problem, the result is better than anything any one person could come up with on their own. When groups come together to address specific challenges, they call the results innovations. Innovation has taken mankind into space and allowed him to peer into the farthest reaches of the galaxy. It has provided a way for an individual to study on every continent simultaneously, and shrunk the size of a computer so it fits in the palm of your hand. The principle of synergy is defined as "the interaction or cooperation of two or more organizations, substances, or other agents to produce a combined effect greater than the sum of their separate effects."[3] *There is power in unity.* No matter

---

[3] "Synergy–definition of synergy in English/Oxford Dictionaries," Oxford Dictionaries/English, accessed August 3, 2017, https://en.oxforddictionaries.com/definition/synergy.

how smart, talented, industrious, or driven you are—you will always have a better result if you partner with (and stay partnered with) someone else.

Honor the Time Required for the Project

Our society has provided a false sense that *everything* can be attained *immediately*. This microwave mentality has invaded every single part of our lives. Time is the most crucial ingredient in securing success. You must devote time and attention if you wish to attain status and longevity. My grandfathers' wisdom came from the same spring of knowledge. One of them was a Ford-certified mechanic and the other was a farmer and a sleeping-car porter. They both said that the processes they mastered in life and work had time frames connected to them. If you brought your car to Ab Mason, he would tell you how long he estimated it would take to complete the repairs or maintenance. This assessment was based on his many years of experience, the condition of the automobile (also assessed by his trained eye), his training in this particular field, and his confidence in his ability to do the job. If you asked Eli Stinson when the collard greens or tomatoes he planted would be ready for Sunday supper, he would tell you almost to the day when he could pick those tomatoes and greens. After all their years, they understood how long it all took. Their understanding was based on their many years of experience, their training in this particular field, and their confidence in their ability to do the job. Neither would ever have advocated the idea that time could be manipulated to serve your impatience. If you wanted your car properly repaired or maintained, it took time. If you wanted the most delicious vegetables, it took time: the part that my grandfather invested, and the bulk of the process orchestrated by God in growing those crops.

We hate this idea today, but there are no shortcuts to depth of character. It is built over time and through trial. Our character does not grow quickly. Some of its most important pieces require a great deal of time. Patience and trust are both examples of strengths that grow as relationships persevere in difficulties. Other character traits, such as kindness and mercy, also require time to have their full effect. In fact, all fruit requires time to grow and become strong in a person's life.

Examples of Poor Construction

Today's newscasts provide an abundance of examples of folks who, plain and simple, missed the mark. Their foundations contained massive cracks that were later identified by the way the "buildings" in their lives were falling down around their ears. Ironically, when asked, these folks believed they had taken all the necessary precautions in making their building sound and secure! So what really happened? In each and every case they violated their internal control mechanism. They *knew* that what they were doing violated their foundational principles. They *knew* that the materials they were using were substandard. They *knew* that they were violating the principle of time. They *knew* that they were walking alone, excluding help and expert input. The results were expected: failure. The picture above is what happens when "knowing" doesn't equate to "doing."

The same is true when we are building our lives. We lengthen the ropes of our lives to make room for a greater-sized effort. If this is done without strengthening our supports, we will overextend ourselves and move beyond our abilities. We compromise the strength of these supports by ignoring our foundational principles and the fundamental processes of building. When we test the strength of the supports that hold up our lives, we must be honest with ourselves. The United States Army Corps of Engineers exists to solve many of the nation's engineering problems. This group is regarded as one of the best solutions to building problems. Why? Because their vision, mission, work ethic, research, and development are all tied to a single subject. This is the same singular kind of focus that we must have in building our lives. The unmovable core ideals for success in the building cycle are clear:

- Planning must be done in consultation with the very best authorities available. Wise counsel is effective and worthwhile, so the first step is to assess yourself. What knowledge, skills, and abilities do you possess? Take that assessment and work with mentors that by way of their experience are able to teach you. With their input, come up with a single cohesive plan. And take your time!

- Choose the materials that will form your life wisely. All your choices affect you. The people you hang out with and the books you read influence you. So does where you go to school and the activities you choose to spend your time on. Both your short- and long-term planning, and what you use to feed and sustain your curiosity, shape your life. All these pursuits, while appearing to be independent and separate, work together to form a singular lens through which a person views the world, and is seen by the world in turn. Inspect these areas and make sure you are making wise choices. Change those that are out of line. If you have trouble with this, get help by reviewing these areas with someone you trust.

- Those who influence your life can be viewed as a team of mentors. There will be many members of this ever-changing team in your life. There must be a constant and ongoing selection and placement of them as they are responsible for constructing "you." Some members will be with you for most of your construction, while others will only be needed for a single task. The two goals of the team are to assemble the very best minds and hearts for the work at hand, and pour this corporate knowledge into the building cycle. As this progresses, more skilled and visionary team members are required. Do not settle for just anyone! You are worth it! Invest in the very best this world has to offer.
- The costs (resources, personnel, approvals, and time) must be assessed at each and every stage as we build. Just as you were not born with a deep knowledge of accounting, so you will not develop world-class skills dealing with people overnight. The foundational principles (chapter one) give birth to a wide range of thoughts that are used throughout the building of your life.

This chapter's test has been presented as if men and women were born with a clear sense of where they were going, what they were intended to accomplish, who they were to associate with, and why any of this matters. In truth, it can take us a  long time to understand the importance of building character and finding our purpose. On top of that, the reality of building your life, expanding its borders as you go along, and aligning your resources with the task at hand takes work—hard work! It is when we do not pay attention to this ongoing building process that we lose sight of the expanse of the whole project. A single miscalculation may result in an extension of weeks or months for just one little phase of the building cycle. Strengthen your stakes (foundational structure and integrity) before you lengthen your ropes (expand your life).

When in doubt the Army Corps of Engineers motto holds true: *Essayons!* (French for "Let us try!")

"Through deeds, not words, we are *building strong.*" – U.S. Army Corps of Engineers

Stoke the Fire

1. What materials make up your life? Have these materials been storm-rated? What was the result?

2. This chapter highlights the instant gratification nature of our society; we want everything NOW! What is worth waiting for in your mind's eye?

3. We live in a world in which we often make things up as we go along. Are you guilty of not sitting down and planning where you wish to go, what you wish to do, and how you wish to live the rest of your life?

4. The Lone Ranger attitude is alive and well in many of us. Do you surround yourself with people/friends who will make you better, bitter, or bothered?

5. So now you have a plan, you have resources, you have surrounded yourself with people to assist you. Are you finally ready for success? What else do you need?

6. Bonus: In the building trade, you need a license to build a building. What qualifications do you possess that will enable you to build the building that is "you"?

TEST 3

MIRROR, MIRROR: YOU WERE DESIGNED TO SUCCEED

Our childhood literature would not be complete without *Snow White and the Seven Dwarfs*. According to scholars, this story is presented, with little variation, in most cultures around the globe. It depicts a not-so-nice stepmother who is obsessed with being the fairest maiden in the land. Her self-absorption leads to the abuse of her child, betrayal, a murder-for-hire scheme, a child fleeing the home for safety reasons, an actual murder, ongoing cover-ups, and eventually the power of love conquering all. Many analyses of this story have pointed to a single point: the wicked stepmother's unrealistic and negative self-image fueled all of her negative actions. She was not OK with who she was. She did not believe she was acceptable. Therefore, she had to be the "fairest in the land" according to external comparisons. The horrific part of this fairy tale is that in the United States this story is still being played out in real life, movies, television, video games, more stories, and the untapped imagination of multiple generations. Many people are not comfortable in their own skin. Therefore they are constantly trying to reach a place where they feel better about themselves, where they can look in that mirror and have peace. Unfortunately, the path they choose to get to this place is destructive to themselves and others. Because they are not rooted and grounded in the fact that they are loved by their heavenly Father, they are ever searching for acceptance and approval from others, or trying to make themselves feel better through the many addictions the world offers. All of these behaviors are rooted in what they see in that mirror. How do you see yourself? Are you aware of your worth as a human being? Can you rest deep within because you know you are valuable and loved?

**The Price Paid
for Your Choice
(Something
or Nothing)**

ARE YOU WILLING TO PAY THE PRICE?

Fosdick reflected on the United States' loss of absolutes: "Human life itself is not sacred—they murder for a song. Truth is not sacred—they lie with ease. Friendship is not sacred—they betray their own without a qualm." We live in a world where our self-respect and self-esteem are often not anchored to anything solid. They are ever-changing, floating amid the pre-vailing currents in a person's life. This is the result of many factors, but most notably, failure in the first two tests of character we just covered. They have no priorities or foundational principles, and they have not placed any stock in building their lives. Their building projects are still on the proverbial drawing board. They do not have any sense of identity in the first place!

A byproduct of the loss of foundational principles is the belief that your life does not matter and has no value. How sad, and how untrue! At the time of writing this book you cannot turn on a television without seeing the battle between "Black Lives Matter" and the "All Life Matters" movements. These two ideas were birthed by the public shootings of young men of color. This text is not designed to argue this point and its impor-tance. The value of every human life is unfathomable! This fact, however, has been lost in the many discussions of what is important to our society. Our children grow up not really under-standing what goes into determining their worth. Thus, their actions are immediately separated from the foundational prin-ciples that should give them guidance. When a person pays nothing for an item it stands to reason that it is worthless. Yet when a great price is paid for something, we say it is priceless. We should remind every person we meet that their life matters, that it was paid for with riches that cannot be calculated, and that what they do with their life is therefore of the greatest importance. We all share this responsibility. Jesus Christ was the ultimate payment for our very lives. God paid our outstanding debt with his Son's life, so that we could become the women and men He had originally designed. I understand that there are some that may stumble over that last statement. I would add the following: Without a system of belief, you are left to operate from your core nature—unbridled, undisciplined, and unreliable. And the truth is that we have a God who loves us and whom we can trust. With God's help, we can do so much better than we can on our own. With God's help, we can excel.

The Real Litmus Test

When chemists want to determine the composition of an item, they test the substance to see what comprises its core components. When human beings want to determine  what they are made of, they only need to observe their behaviors. What we do on a routine basis will demonstrate the priorities we have established. Our behavior also indicates areas where we need further development. This is the portion of this book where several disclaimers must be made. Your life is of immeasurable value. The difference between the dirt that you may currently see, and the gold that others see in you, is a matter of knowing the difference between the two. There is no such thing as a lost cause. There is not a single individual who cannot make a positive contribution to our world. The key point here is that they must *want to contribute*. The power of choice is the greatest force on the planet; it is the central driving force, connecting a person's beliefs to their actions.

Once you have determined what someone is made of, then you need to simply ask them: "What do you want to do with these materials?" We are our brother's keeper. In fact, the decline of our society is the result of the alienation of our fellow man and his development from our own lives. It was morally wrong, once upon a time, to allow the less fortunate, the sick, the disenfranchised, the burnt-out, the struggling, and the wounded to go through life without receiving a helping hand. It was also a matter of duty to look out for those who had not progressed to the level you now occupied. How different our society would look if overnight all citizens of our nation began to care for one another. These pivotal points of our foundational principles can be defined and refined. They will not, however, compose themselves. They require our concerted attention. Only then can we change our culture for the better again.

Your Ongoing Obituary

I have experienced mind-numbing loss in the last several years. My immediate and extended family has graduated to glory in numbers for which I was not prepared. The ironic thing about death is that there is very little you can do to prepare for it, other than enjoy every single day with those in your life! Every funeral service I attended included the same core information: who the person was, what made their life remarkable, and who they left behind. Self-esteem is built upon the reality that your worth is not determined by what gifts you were given at birth or along your journey, but what type of gift you have become to your family, your community, your nation, and the world. We hear of superstars, public officials, church leaders, and other prominent citizens being remembered for the many things that they accomplished during their lives. It is logical, to some, to believe that without a notable title, a prominent family, or a success or two, your life is void of meaning. Nothing could be further from the truth! Your life is a reflection of the principles you held, regardless of what you accomplished. I cannot tell you the number of times that folks I didn't know praised the accomplishments of one of my family members. These unsolicited reports of random kindness were inspirational and informational. My family made such an impact on these people that their very lives were changed. During my mother's funeral, there were so many of these testimonies of her kindness that it seemed staged. The truth of my mother's life was that she sowed good seeds into every single person she met. Each person was a new and fertile field into which her love could be placed. At the end of her time on earth, each seed was paraded for all to see: now fully grown as plants of love.

The Seeds We Sow

We are what we think, what we surround ourselves with, and what we strive to become. If we devalue ourselves from the beginning, our perceived net worth must overcome a substantial barrier before it grows out of that negative shell. Our self-esteem and our self-conceit are at war every single minute of every single day. If the picture we have of ourselves is distorted, or otherwise maladjusted, we may fall prey to a wrong assessment. This is the bottom line for many confused souls who cannot seem to separate who they really are from their self-imposed opinions. Failing this test means one simple thing: You may never believe the reports that say you are destined for greatness. One example of this is the child who is fed a steady diet of ridicule, demeaning labels, cruel put-downs, incessant teasing, heartless comparisons to failed individuals, and criminal verbal attacks. This child's belief in his own abilities, self-confidence, self-worth, and faith in a future have all been compromised. This child's concept of hope rests in what he *cannot* do! This messy baggage must be unpacked before the truth of the core of his self-esteem can be disclosed. Albert Einstein was recorded as saying, "I have no special talents. I am only passionately curious."[4] The highest honor we may bestow upon our fellow men is to affirm the godlike qualities they possess: wonder, inquisitiveness, creativity, introspection, honesty, humility, and the awareness that we will never have all of the answers. This is the key: Live like there is no tomorrow, while being thankful for the contributions you have been allowed to give today.

---

[4] Albert Einstein, "Sample Chapter for Einstein, A; Calaprice, A., ed.: The Expanded Quotable Einstein.," Princeton University, accessed August 3, 2017, http://press.princeton.edu/chapters/s6908.html.

Stoke the Fire

1. In many ways we are the sum total of everything we have thought, read, experienced, and were taught. Why then do we so often question the usefulness of this vast library of information to define who we were destined to become?

2. Death is a reality for which few of us are prepared. What are you doing now to give substance to the story that will become your eulogy?

3. There are a great many souls that are completely lost in the search for who God made them to be. What are you doing to discover the hidden gifts, talents, and meaning stored in your DNA?

4. Our self-image often is the limiting factor in our lives. We do not succeed, because we don't think we can succeed. We cannot attain, because we believe we cannot attain. What strategies are you putting in place to arrest the thoughts that may limit you, or hold you hostage?

5. Albert Einstein spoke a profound truth when he said, **"I have no special talents. I am only passionately curious."** How can you change the culture around you to support those who may see their unique vantage point of life as only ordinary, because they do not learn, or think, the way "we" do?

6. Bonus: We are often allergic to our own success. What are the core components needed to embrace being successful beyond your thoughts or dreams?

TEST 4

THE PERSON BEHIND THE MASK: HARNESSING THE POWER TO SEE THE INVISIBLE

I like superheroes, those who keep their identity hidden behind masks. Their alter egos provided them the ability to "hide in plain sight." Their alter egos also allowed them to appear normal to the unsuspecting public. It was the rare, and often beloved, person who discovered the true identity of these superheroes: a trust they were sworn to secrecy for the life of the person (or at least the television show). This test is equally as cryptic: seeing the invisible reality in the person behind the mask. Imagine an old, worn, weather-beaten rocking chair on the front porch of a house. The house, by comparison, is freshly painted, and architecturally modern. When the homeowner is asked what is that on the front porch, they respond with a heavy sigh, a huge smile, and a sparkle in their eye. The person asking the question may be a bit taken aback. In the questioner's eyes, it is just a rocking chair. To the homeowner, however, there are a thousand memories, discussions, decisions, tears, laughter, people, and indescribable love bound up in that chair. What is the difference between these two people? One can only see what is in front of them, the tangible, while the other has harnessed the ability to see the invisible.

The Reality of Your Composition

With over 100 billion neurons, you are made of

the most sophisticated network of sensors, processors, and computer interfaces the world has ever known. Your mind is far more complicated than any machine ever developed. You, as a mechanism, are so complicated that 3,000 years of study have only begun to decode the very basics of your operation. We cannot even reproduce a conscious thought. Since this technology is beyond our wildest imagination and light-years ahead of our current ability to decode, how can we harness the mind in order to see things that are not? Doing this is actually part of the more basic operations of the human brain. We are born ready to store, associate, and categorize countless points of stimulation. We then attach these points of stimulations to "triggers" that serve as keyboard shortcuts (like "Alt-F7"), allowing us to access multiple images, smells, memories, ideas, tastes, emotions, and experiences quickly. In real time, this phenomenon is experienced rather than described. A child walks into a room and smells the lingering presence of cologne, triggering a thousand points of stimulation of a parent. An adult enters a house during the holidays and smells the aroma of pies baking in the oven, triggering a flood of past holidays, laughter, and faces. A young woman stands at the very spot where she experienced her first kiss, triggering a flood of home movies now playing in her head. These are examples of how the invisible makes its way into our everyday lives.

The Search for Transparency

When we realize that the rhyme and reason behind these triggers is beyond our ability to understand, we may stop looking for a

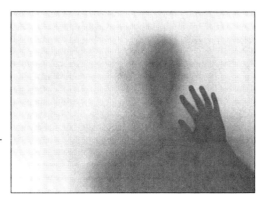

connection. Once we have reached this frustration stage, we resign ourselves to the reality that we have these triggers, that the triggers will pop up at the most unexpected times, and that they are often the result of unknown and uncontrollable stimuli. They just happen. Human beings are curious by nature. We question why things are the way they are, why people do the things they do, why events play out as they do. We question the relationships between things, and between us and things. Most importantly, we question why some things have meaning and importance while others do not. We appreciate and value those individuals who are able to see into this invisible realm regularly. We give even more importance and value to those who allow us to see into their invisible realm with them. This journey into their being, this transparency, is the greatest privilege that someone may bestow on another human being. It is in this process that one person allows another to learn and experience who they really are. They share themselves.

Is the search for transparency a deliberate, premeditated act? I would say yes. A person takes off their mask on purpose, and for a purpose. The purpose is so others will see the person's true nature, and so others can share in the thousands of triggers that make that person unique. They are allowing you to see behind the mask. Once unmasked, we often ask the question: "Are our superheroes still super?"

Will People Still "Like" Me?

With your mask off, completely uncovered for the whole world to see, we are faced with our greatest inse-curities. For most, this begins with denial, not acceptance. Will others accept who we really are? Will they still like me? It is easy to like a superhero! They can fly, stop bullets, look really great in their outfits, and people love them for saving the universe. But human beings are very reluctant to accept the "superpowers" they possess. In fact, we are our own worst enemy. We can single-handedly destroy what has taken a lifetime to create and develop. We will deny what others clearly see. Then we dissolve into a mass of tears and cry, "What have I done?" Fosdick stated that mankind has the ability to look "down, out, and up." We can look down upon created beings that are lower in the order of things (animals, plants, and so on). Man can also look out on his fellow man, and as we have seen, often compare themselves with disastrous results! However, man can also look up. Fosdick said, "Man's distinction is that he can admire, adore; that he is aware of something or someone above him, possessing the right to his devout allegiance; that he can know reverence." It is this upward act of reverence that unlocks the secret of mankind. We are designed to transcend judgment. Because we can look up, we have the power to move to another plane of existence, another dimension, far above where judgment, ridicule, negative barbs of hate, and labels reside. Simply put, the air is too rare, and too thin for these things to exist there. They become oxygen-deprived and expire. However, problems come when we forget to look up, and *choose* to live on the same block as these forces. Then, and only then, are we forced into hand-to-hand combat, defending our own sanity and self-esteem. Too often we lose that battle.

When looking up is a practice, a habit, a way of our life, a subconscious trigger, a reality in all we do then, we will understand transcendence. We will be able to "abide in Christ" with our lives guided and filled with His love and understanding.

Paying the Price for Truthfulness[5]

And ye shall know the truth, and the truth shall make you free.

We are taught as children that "honesty is the best policy." Yet this truth is often met with love taps administered by our parents for admitting to wrongdoing. It does not take long before the love taps birth another lesson: *Some things are best not said.* Any parent will agree that there is nothing worse than knowing that your child is guilty of something and watching him, unsuccessfully, cover up the truth with a lie. These sweet deviations from reality are the cause for most people's gray hair. Love taps are now given in two varieties: one when we tell the truth for wrongdoing, and the other, more memorable version when we lie. This sad dance is carried with us into our pre-teen, teen, young adult, and adult lives. Some learned the lesson and just tell the truth, but others are still swayed by the consequences in determining if the truth, the whole truth, and nothing but the truth, should be shared. You cannot look up if your eyes are on what you are trying to cover up. There are no cover-ups in that rare air up there.

We must train ourselves to only look up. When this practice becomes a pillar of our priorities, a vital part of our foundation, and a central motivator in our everyday lives we will gladly pay the price for missing the mark of untruthfulness. We will look up, and allow lies to fall from us. We will tell the truth, and pay the price for hurting those around us who were hurt by our

---

[5] See John 8:32.

deception. We will safeguard ourselves by making better decisions the next time we come to similar situations. It is powerful to remember that our real superhero status rests in our ability to live with our masks off.

The Fraternity of the Naked

The fraternity of the naked is your church. Composed of like-minded individuals, the local church is a living organism that strives to develop those within its walls, and minister to the community outside its walls at the same time. Equipped with tools to  develop members, spread the message of hope and salvation, and touch lives everywhere, the church is seen by many as a force for good. With all of its qualities the church has one giant flaw—it cannot get out of its own way in failing to look up—thus allowing the same weeds that hamper the growth of individuals to grow in the church too. Wow! Being made up of imperfect human beings, the church is subject to the same traps and pitfalls as its members. When the church forgets that it cannot transcend these negative forces without looking up, it is encumbered by the same difficulties. Fosdick never imagined that the church would devolve into such a state. In his day, the core of character was walked out daily by a person's Christian beliefs. Unfortunately, over time these beliefs have become more like a list of suggestions than a way of life. The good Reverend Fosdick would be most upset.

Our nation is in a state of turmoil. The church may be the only answer our country has left. In spite of its often-diluted message, its failure to reach into the surrounding community, and its alienation of those who are not already "living a good life," the structure of the church is sound. Its principles are battle-tested, and remain relevant to this age. What is missing? YOU! Change is the byproduct of individuals with a commitment to accomplish something different. The only thing the church needs is your upwardly looking self. Coach, teach, train, and mentor those around you to *look up*. If you live focused on God, He will help you minister to others. You will find your words meeting with receptive ears and willing hearts. People around you are having problems learning how to see the invisible. They are reluctant to take off their masks, and just be normal. Their transparency plan is stuck on the drawing board. They are waiting for a voice that tells the story of how an imperfect person made this perfect plan work. They are waiting for you!

Stoke the Fire

1. Similar to the last chapter, we often struggle with protecting our feelings against the perceptions of what others may think of us. Why are we preoccupied with listening to, keeping up with, and the opinions of "the Joneses"?

2. Our very soul longs for a place of safety, where we can just be ourselves. List five people around whom you can truly be yourself? (You may wish to reach out to them, and say thank you!)

3. Each day of our lives there are thousands of sight, sound, smell, and touch triggers that flood our being. How do you manage these many triggers so they form a positive motivator, and not a negative stumbling block?

4. Many strive to reach a level with other people in which there is nothing that separates them from us. What are your biggest obstacles to attaining and maintaining transparency?

5. In the final equation, we are responsible for seeing the vast array of information that is stored in us as human beings. It is as much the unseen, as the seen and known that will determine our final potential. What are you doing to capture the key invisible truths in your life that are needed to equip you for the next best "you"?

6. Bonus: Looking someone in the eye was once a mark of adulthood, honor, and strength. What has happened to our society?

TEST 5

LOVING AND CHERISHING ONE DAY AT A TIME: DO NOT OVERLOOK THE PRESENT!

Each and every day that you find your lungs filled with air, your mind attentive to the many concerns of life, and your spirit engaged in looking up, a choice knocks on the door of your being, and asks: "Have you decided what kind of day you will have?" One of the greatest tests in this book is that of maintaining the privilege of living. Yes, every single day is a privilege for you to be on the earth. There you go again, shaking your head as if I have said something that is not true. This test requires you to believe several things for you to see its worth. You must realize that happiness is a choice and make a decision to grasp it. You must also reject the comfort of wallowing in the "muddy-grubs." I have heard folks speak of their days as though they were a jail sentence. They are just here "serving their time" until they are released to something else: freedom perhaps. I don't know. Meanwhile others embrace the newness of each day as if it were a beautifully wrapped gift topped with a bow. How can these polar opposites coexist? For some, life is a spectrum with good and bad experiences in equal doses. Others discount the good because they feel that it is overshadowed by the immensity of the bad. What an interesting puzzle! Let's get busy putting some pieces in place.

How Many IOUs Do You Have?

We live in a capitalistic society. Do not get this confused with the claims of democracy that fill most textbooks and the airwaves. Capitalism, in part, is defined as the ability to work hard according to a plan, enduring the hard times in the journey, with the expectancy that you can accomplish anything your heart desires. Democracy says that each individual matters, and that each person's voice will be heard. These two concepts are not in conflict with one another. Amazingly, they have worked hand in hand for centuries. So why is there a conflict now? The conflict rests in the emergence of capitalism as a replacement for family values. It has become a driving force from which many of our life's principles are being established. The result is that many of our core ideals have become goal- and business-driven (as if this was not only normal, but had always existed this way). This is not the way it has always been; this is a change, and not a good one. One example is the idea that if you don't reach a certain place in society it is because you have not worked hard enough, did not have a clear and concise plan, or gave up in some way. Your worth and success are measured by how hard you work, how well you plan, and your perseverance. A subtle shift has taken place—you are now evaluated by something you do—not by who you are and what you believe. In the same manner our foundational principles have also shifted, and everything is a result of something we do. We have gathered countless IOUs from life because we believe that it "owes" us something better. We are entitled. Everything depends on our performance.

A middle-aged man sits in the office of his therapist, reviewing the reasons for the feeling of failure he is experiencing:

Man: "Doc, I just can't seem to shake the feeling that my whole life is a failure."

Doctor: "I see. How long have you had this feeling?"

Man: "It started when I was a child, and I wasn't picked for the kickball team."

Doctor: "Was that important to you?"

Man: "It was very important! All of the 'in' crowd was chosen."

Doctor: "And you wanted to be 'in'?"

Man: "I had worked hard to get to that point, Doc!"

Doctor: "I can see where this would frustrate you. How old were you?"

Man: "I had just turned five...I remember it like it was yesterday."

Obviously, this is an oversimplification of a chronic problem—we cannot let go of the things we believe to be central to our happiness: our acceptance with the "in" crowd, promotions, where we live, what we drive, what we wear, who knows us, who we know, our net worth, and a thousand other points of darkness that we have established as important. We live our lives amassing a shopping list of qualifiers that will assure happiness. Rarely do we admit that none of these "treasures" guarantee our happiness. Some few realize that happiness rests in our ability to seize the best each day has to offer, and let go of the remainder. When this is the pattern for our daily existence it is impossible that any day would not yield a bounty of joy.

Deferred Gratification and Other Contradictions of Life

So what's with the marshmallows? Walter Mischel, a Stanford University researcher, began a series of powerful studies in the 1960s. He and his team conducted what would later be coined the "Marshmallow Experiment." The study was brilliant: place a four- to five-year-old child in a private room and place a single marshmallow in front of him. Each child was told that if he did not eat the marshmallow when the researcher left the room, he would be rewarded with a second one later. Got it? One now, or two later. This historic study was the basis for much of the work on trust and deferred gratification. Each of the children was followed for the next forty years. To the surprise of the researchers the study found that children who demonstrated the power to delay had higher SAT scores, lower levels of substance abuse, better responses to stress, better social skills as reported by their parents, and generally better scores in a range of other life measures. In short, they were better-equipped to achieve their goals in life and attain success.

What is your marshmallow? In some areas we are really good at waiting things out, knowing that down the road we will receive double and triple our investment. In other areas we have gobbled up that marshmallow before the door closed behind the researcher! This is the conflict that makes life so filled with uncertainty. We simply do not know that delaying a thing will result in the reward we want. Our society, many of our inner circle, friends, and many of our mentors have counseled us to seize the day: *Carpe diem*! This is the battle cry of a generation that moves from challenge to challenge, job to job, event to event, based solely on how it benefits them. Sound familiar? We wake up most days only concerned with what is underway for that day, and we forget about the long-term projects that require daily input to complete.

The book you hold in your hand was twenty-plus years in the making. OK, so some of that time was spent procrastinating (an earlier chapter), and some of that time was spent questioning my ability to write (another earlier chapter), and some of that time was just wasted (the denial I mentioned before). So what really happened, Doc? I had a great idea, I was motivated to do it, but I did not redeem each and every day. I was not concerned with delayed rewards; I simply did not see procrastination slowly killing my dreams. I took no pleasure in the days that I only wrote a sentence, or no words at all. I squandered the miracle of each day, and reaped the horrible reward of being unfulfilled. Unfortunately, I punished myself for the days that did not meet my expectations. This refusal to embrace the privilege of living resulted in the greatest hindrance to progress: self-condemnation. How many of us are stuck in this cycle of destruction at our own hands? Do not despair! As you read these words, construct a mental stop sign in your mind. Decide right now to not let this toxic habit continue in your life. Wash these poisons from your soul by letting yourself off the proverbial hook. Allow yourself to enjoy each day and do what you can, trusting God to bring all to completion. You will find that your tomorrow will be filled with amazing possibilities because of this decision.

"Life Ain't Been No Crystal Stair"

In the timeless poem "Mother to Son" by Langston Hughes, the above line is penned as an example of the hardness that must be endured in the course of one's life. The premise of the poem is both simple and complex: Life requires that we give attention to the many things that may come against you. The mother in the poem speaks of a mythical set of stairs containing obstacles like "tacks," "splinters," "torn-up boards," and "places with no carpet—bare." The mother also gives navigational insight from her own journey for the son to take to heart: "climb on," "reach landings," "turn corners," "go in the dark" (where there has never been light), and then later he is told: don't set down, don't fall, and don't turn back. The first time I read this poem I was confused. We had carpeted steps in our home. My mother was a fanatic about making sure that things were maintained. But I was really young when I first read it. The lessons I have learned, the things I have seen, and the people I have spoken with since that time have made this poem a real help for my life. In this chapter we are learning to see both the visible and the invisible, and use this ability to see the power in others. This poem is an amazing example of the invisible becoming reality. Let's unpack some of the key lessons we can learn from "Mother to Son" by Langston Hughes. Perhaps you would enjoy reading it in its entirety:

Well, son, I'll tell you:
Life for me ain't been no crystal stair.
It's had tacks in it,
And splinters,
And boards torn up,
And places with no carpet on the floor—
Bare.
But all the time
I'se been a-climbin' on,
And reachin' landin's,
And turnin' corners,
And sometimes goin' in the dark
Where there ain't been no light.
So boy, don't you turn back.

Don't you set down on the steps
'Cause you finds it's kinder hard.
Don't you fall now—
For I'se still goin', honey,
I'se still climbin',
And life for me ain't been no crystal stair.[6]

The Wisdom of the Elders

In each conversation with those older than me, I am reminded that wisdom is a priceless element that is best shared with those that are prepared to receive it. We often roll our eyes, become impatient, or do not value the time spent with our elders. In fact, the time spent with our elders is often seen as a chore as if it were a punishment for doing something wrong! Nothing could be further from the truth. Within the weathered clay containers of these men and women resides knowledge and insight, prophetic musings and pictures, global truths and patterns. Many of them are eager to share the treasure trove they gained throughout their lives, but it's only available to you if you have the discipline to understand the rules. Rules? Yes, there are rules. There are always rules.

1. **No conversation with your elders is by chance**. God has ordained us to have these men and women in our lives. Each represents a specific area of development within our life's journey. He set these precious times up for us. Enjoy them.
2. **No conversation should be engaged without full attention**. You will never know what life lesson will be shared, and how these lessons will change your very existence. You will miss something if you are distracted. Pay attention!

---

[6] Langston Hughes, *Selected Poems of Langston Hughes*, New York: Vintage Books, 1990, 187.

3. **Elders demand the highest order of respect**. If you do not know Miss Manners, get to know her! Our elders demand not only our full attention, but also the greatest care. It is not OK to consider them your peers, just random people, or those who do not deserve every social grace. Caution should be used to avoid rude and disrespectful speech. In a nutshell, take care that you are gracious and respectful. They deserve your respect and consideration.

4. **Elders will provide you with priceless jewels—protect them!** If you were given a five-carat diamond ring, I doubt you would lay it next to your kitchen sink while you were doing dishes, or on your nightstand when you went to bed. You'd carefully put it into a jewelry box where it would be safe. The same should be true of the words that elders impart. It is our duty and obligation to take these priceless downloads and provide a place of safety and security for them too. Only then will you have them available, library style, as you journey. Journal what is shared with you! Think about what they share.

5. **If you miss the wisdom of your elders, the lessons may be lost forever.** Consider this fact! The wisdom that elders possess will pass with them if it is not shared with someone beforehand. In time, our elders move on from this temporal existence. When they do, they will take everything not bestowed on others with them. The immensity of this task should not be missed. Make time for them!

The Map of the Elders

"Mother to Son" represents a map that the attentive young un' will construct from actual elders in their life. Like the mother in the poem, our elders give us high-level insights into what is required to make our journey easier. Our elders cannot live our lives. They can only share the insight and wisdom that they have amassed during their journey up the staircase. Many of you are saying, "Doc, every journey is different. What worked for one surely cannot work for another. There is no map that is one-size-guides-most!" Not so! Do not discredit their wisdom! Those who have gone before us left signs so that those who follow would know the way. Only recently has it been necessary to give GPS coordinates to find a location. Once you know what to look for, the signs of our elders are hidden in plain sight! The truths they have to share are universal.

The Obstacles the Elders Faced

The obstacles listed in this poem don't seem particularly dangerous, but they would certainly be a problem for you if you were climbing a staircase: Look out for nails, splinters, decaying boards, worn parts of life, paths without light, and losing your way. The more we think about these issues the more we can apply them to our lives. Knowing that those older than we are went through particular troubles and problems helps us. We can see that they came through these "rough patches" successfully. They can tell us how they did that. We can gain in wisdom and understanding by sitting at their feet because they will point to the strategies that helped them through their hard times. They will tell us about their relationships with their children, their parents and their grandparents. They will share their faith and how it was tested and grew. They will tell us about the power of prayer, and how God met them in it. Every story, every discussion, every warning, every family joke, is like gold: It is part of our inheritance. We do not have to make all the same mistakes that they made, and we can rejoice in their victories. We can walk carefully and learn from them. Their stories become our stories.

Our elders provide us with crown jewels that they still wear proudly. Sad to say, their words are falling on the ears of a generation that may see Mother Alice, Dr. Sewell, Bishop Whitelocke,

Dr. Artman, Big Momma, Nana, or Paw Paw as irrelevant. They are waiting to share their wealth with our generation. We need to open our hearts and our ears to their voices.

Check Your Settings

We are halfway through this text and many of you may believe that this book is about taking folks to the proverbial wood-shed. Nothing could be further from the truth. When I read the original *Twelve Tests of Character*, it changed my life, and it was not because I passed every test. It changed my life because I failed most of the tests. It was sobering to look at mistake after mistake, and know that it was up to me to do something different. God had gifted me in many ways: I had a great upbringing, excellent schools, great teachers and mentors, strong intellect, plenty of opportunities, a strong spiritual foundation, and so much more! Yet somewhere along the path I had lost my way. I was operating beneath the standards I had set for myself, as well as those that were set for me. In today's technobabble, I needed to do a hard reset of my core operating system. This meant addressing the items that were threatening to take control. Wow, that was intense! With some honest assessments and hard work, I did what was nec-essary to address this reset: counseling, changing my reading diet, changing my friends, getting back into church and living in dependence on God, learning to lead with love, and setting distinct priorities. What a relief that was!

As good as the reset seemed to be, I was ignorant about the system's maintenance. What happens to a car that is in peak condition when it is not maintained? It begins to dete-riorate over time, systems begin to fail, and soon you need major repairs. The same is true of us. A system reset is only as good as the maintenance you put in place afterward. There are numerous diagnostic tools that can help you take care of your car. God has provided the same internal mechanisms for us. They may not ding or blink, but they do provide you with a clear indicator that everything is not functioning normally. It would be in our best interest to heed their warnings!

This chapter is filled with nuggets of truth that allow you the ability to appreciate every day, and understand the awesome privilege it is to live in it. This realization may be the most significant point in your journey. Your life is a special gift that is given only to you. Line up one hundred people, and you will have one hundred stories of where "here" is. Ask the same one hundred people how they got *here*, and you will find that there are similarities and themes that transcend age, gender, socioeconomic standing, church denomination, ethnicity, and background. We are all internally guided by motivators that push us forward. These motivators, collectively, represent who we are. Our internal drives are a vast collection of things we have picked up, casually noticed, and expressly learned from our elders. There's also things we learn from what they do *not* teach us! The construction of these internal drives is not always positive. This process can be painful, is often the result of traumatic experiences, and sometimes the only lasting benefit we receive from an otherwise forgettable experience. Robert F. Kennedy, in his speech announcing the assassination of Dr. Martin Luther King, Jr., cited the words of the Greek scholar Aeschylus:

> **"Even in our sleep, pain which cannot forget falls drop by drop upon the heart, until in our own despair, against our will, comes wisdom through the awful grace of God."**

Stoke the Fire

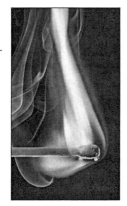

1. This chapter speaks to the com-
    plexity of relationships. What can
    we do to foster an openness in
    which communication across the
    generations is routine?

2. What really makes you happy? If
    you could not answer this question
    easily, what are you going to do
    so that you may uncover the true motivator deep in
    your being?

3. Today is often not valued as the ONLY answer; we have
    tomorrow, next week, and months to come. Redeeming
    each and every day often becomes a huge under-
    taking. What changes will you make to insure you can
    get the most productivity out of tomorrow possible?

4. Our elders are a wonderful source of direction, knowl-
    edge, instruction, and inspiration. List five elders whom
    you are inspired to schedule time with based on this
    chapter. What things are holding you back from calling
    them (if any)?

5. We operate within multiple systems at all times. What
    measures do you have in place that give you the infor-
    mation needed to maintain the high performance of
    your systems?

6. Bonus: For many of us it is time to address the really hard
    things that are not working in our lives. Who is a part
    of your accountability group who will help you reach
    this point?

TEST 6

THE GREEN GRASS TEST: LEARNING TO MIND ONE'S OWN BUSINESS

People take great satisfaction in looking at their finely manicured lawns. It is green, plush, and edged to perfection. Some are only satisfied if their lawn bests their neighbors. The deeper we sink into the quicksand of this thinking, the more important it is to prove the superiority of our lawn. Really pathetic, huh? Yet, we as a society are tied to this test in ways we do not want to admit. Are our clothes from the "right" designer? Is the make of our car on the "must have" list for the year? Is our child's school exclusive enough? Are we filling our lives with the latest "trending" gadgets? This chapter will cover a most overlooked test; how to manage yourself.

For Whom Does the Grass Matter?

Our preoccupation with what other people think of us is as old as time. Jealousy, comparisons, and competitions push

us to get more stuff. As things became easier to acquire, the fight for these trinkets became more intense. People were no longer at ease with enough. Or more accurately, enough was never enough. We have become insatiable in our desire to possess stuff, compare our stuff with someone else's, and acquire more stuff as quickly as possible.

Our thirst for status has fueled our perception that our lives were inadequate. Not once in this process do we stop and use the old tool of introspection. In a perfect world, the "grass" only matters to the owner of the "grass," and the owner of the "grass" is only concerned with how the "grass" has progressed since last year. In the real world, the focus was taken off the "grass" and placed on us. The man in the mirror preoccupies our thoughts and plans. What's in it for me (WIFM)? What do I get out of the deal? How will I benefit? Sadly, this level of self-absorption is destroying our sense of community. We discount it as irrelevant to our lives.

Can You Face Your Toughest Opponent?

There comes a point in each and every life when you realize the battle is not without, but within. You, my dear reader, are the biggest obstacle to both your destiny and the fulfillment of your purpose. As long as the "grass" even matters to you, there is a deep problem. The problem is that you have not faced and defeated your greatest opponent—yourself. The part of us that makes up our feelings, emotions, desires, and sense of contentment is a seasoned adversary. This soul realm has defeated, derailed, divided, and destroyed many an individual. Our newspaper headlines are filled with the stories of people who have decided to allow their soul realm to rule and reign in their lives. The result is failure. Our soul realm is not interested in just bankrupting one part of us; it is poised and focused to rule every part of us. Get some paper and take this very simple test:

1. Write down the three things that take most of your time.
2. Write down the three things that you spend most of your money on.
3. Write down the five things you must have to be successful.
4. Write down three people whom you admire for their success.

How did you do? Let's find out. The first question reflects whether or not your most important resource lines up with your priorities (see chapter 1). The second question asks if your financial resources line up with your priorities. The third question reflects your ability to put priorities and foundational items into practice. The last question is crucial, as it ponders the list of those on which you secretly pattern your life. If you found that your list is misaligned with your priorities, your foundational principles, and your true icons of success, you may wish to reassess where you actually are. Remember, it is necessary for you to be honest with yourself if you are to make genuine progress.

Possession versus Ownership

We have many traits that define who we are, what we do, and for what we will be known. When we are faced with the reality brought about by our inner stuff, it is clear that how we view this stuff is very important. Many deny that they have problems, issues, and quirks that hold them back from staying in their lane. They may possess a treasure trove of maladies, but they do not *own* a single one! Yes, they are the CEO, chairman of the board, and chief stockholder of the Millionaire Denial Club. The sole purpose of this club is to make problems someone else's fault. Got caught gossiping? That was because "they" asked for advice. Got caught speaking ill of someone? That was because "they" had it coming. Got caught giving unsolicited advice? That was because "they" seemed lost. This person did not possess the control needed so that "they" could navigate toward success. In truth, "they" were further hindered by someone who did not own their shortcomings. Almost every twelve-step program in the world begins with the premise that you must own your issues (Hi! My name is _____, and I am _____.)

We Build from the Inside Out

The key to any renovation project is to have an approved set of plans that will result in the outcome you desire. Our lives are governed by the same exact process. Change does not occur because plans are not made. Plans are not made because the homeowner either does not know how to complete the plans, or believes the scope of work does not require plans. The homeowner's confusion rests squarely in their denial of what issues impact them directly. True change takes place when the homeowner sees the deplorable condition of their inner self, and makes up their mind to renovate. With a made-up mind, the "home-owner" begins the massive process of making changes.

The true nature of change is that it leaves very little time to be concerned with someone else's issues and agendas. We pray for these folks and keep our mind on our own work. We understand that every available resource we have is necessary for the task at hand. This, and only this, will result in excellence of outcome. If we spend our time poking into other people's business, we will fail in our own. That is not acceptable, so we focus. We keep our eyes on our own plate.

Stoke the Fire

1. The grass is not greener because it is on the other side of the fence. The grass is greener because it is well cared for! How are you taking care of you, and not worrying about the comparison to others?

2. I use the adage in my classrooms, "Do what you have to do, so you can do what you want to do." What are you doing to ensure that you are a priority, even with other folks pulling on your limited resources?

3. Our generation has majored in living for today. What will you do to expand your mind beyond yourself?

4. We are our biggest obstacle. What has this chapter instilled in you that can now be used as a tool to address yourself? How will you get the strength to walk this out daily?

5. HGTV and other do-it-yourself channels show us how to make home improvement projects easy. Our lives are not seen in the same way. What are you going to do with your internal house that will lead to changing your status?

6. Bonus: What does change mean to you? Are you excited that you are changing? Why, or why not?

TEST 7

AUTHORITY: THE BASICS OF OBEDIENCE

Harry Emerson Fosdick wrote, "One of our most venerated and farseeing citizens recently remarked that in his eighty years of active life, associated with some of the most stirring events in the commonwealth, he had never seen such an orgy of lawlessness as that through which we are living now." As we now know, Fosdick's friend was horribly wrong in his assessment. The lawless life of the early twentieth century has devolved into a much worse cesspool of murder, theft, corruption, lies, immorality, cheating, dishonor, and denial of civil and religious authority. Twenty-first century society boasts about this disregard as a sign of a changing generation. They even think it is changing for the better! We are on the verge of a total collapse of the principles that this country was founded upon. Yet, there is no public outcry for this historic failure.

The Individual, Society at Large, and Organizations

The challenge to our current society is to purposefully build into every life the character necessary to support both healthy personal growth and morality. There has been a decided breakdown of the individual, our organizations, and our society at large in curbing this downward spiral in standards and integrity. Fosdick was aware that for learning to take place foundational principles must be introduced to the individual, echoed by organizations where the individual has membership, and fashioned as vital by the general community. This was the educational standard of his time. My, how times have changed!

Today's technology, in all its demonstrations, has made isolation an acceptable state of being. The new educational model is that the individual will grasp concepts that interest them, at their own pace, and when they are ready to learn the lessons. Character continues to be relegated to the bottom of the list of important topics. Character and integrity are also not terribly important items societally. Genuine change is only possible by reconstituting all three levels of influence. This is not an easy task. In fact, Fosdick spent his entire series demonstrating the responsibility of the individual to wake up, and take a stand. This was a difficult proposition in the 1920s, and it may be seemingly impossible in the twenty-first century.

Who Is Really in Charge?

Control rests with the individual. We may optimistically claim that our laws, home training, or even socially accepted conduct rule the day, but the truth is that each person makes up their mind about what is acceptable to them on a daily basis. This situational ethics dilemma results in moving targets of morality. Folks are applauded for not getting caught. So the next generation is trained in this central thought: just don't get caught. The counterargument (Just don't do it!) is not only unpopular, it is never mentioned! Why?

Making Your Own Rules

Our society challenges the reality of approved rules. You may ask, "If the rules are approved what is there to challenge?" On the surface that is a valid and poignant question. Remember, we are teaching generations to "not get caught." This speaks to a sinister subliminal message: all laws, rules, codes of conduct, and socially accepted mores can be ignored or disobeyed. Just don't get caught! Individuals carefully construct a set of personal guidelines that work for them. Everything from breaking the speed limit to cheating on income taxes, reporting all sources of income to taking supplies from work, lying to avoid a commitment to gross exaggeration to get a specific job are everyday occurrences. We live in a land of situational ethics.

The Inward Desire to Rule

At the core of this situational conundrum is our unbridled desire to rule. We not only wish to be in charge of our lives, we also want to be in charge of every possible outcome in our lives. This allows us to craft an existence that matches our mental images. What we have forgotten is that most of these mental images are delusions. This is not to say that mankind should not have dreams, aspirations, and positive plans. We should, but this list gives way to shortcuts, the easy paths, and instant gratification. Most people understand that their dreams will require focus and hard work. This is in stark contradiction to our self-delusions. We cannot expect world changers if the standard underneath the work changes on a daily basis. Where does this misguided view of one's self come from?

The Dysfunction of the Family

Research done by Gerson and Torres[7] and earlier, Gerson[8] alone, has shown that the failure of our family structure has directly contributed to the inability of individuals to navigate the world in which they live. The majority of our citizens do not possess the skills to attain the legitimate dreams they have within their hearts. In earlier chapters we have spoken of failure to plan, delayed gratification, a need to establish goals and foundational principles, required inspections of your life work, and the necessity of grasping the invisible things of the divine. When Fosdick wrote *The Twelve Tests of Character,* all of these issues began with parents teaching their children (and those whom they "adopted" as their own). Inspired parents looked at their families as a legacy they were building, and part of their *legacy* required them to pour themselves into their children. The old adage was true: "You (children) will build your life upon the foundation that I have built." Family businesses, a family profession, and linked family professions were commonplace during the twentieth century. The twenty-first century, however, has brought a greater diversity to families. You may still see children following in their parents' footsteps, but normally they are drifting far from the family ship. This is happening for a number of reasons:

Children Are in Open and Constant Rebellion

In the mid- to late 1960s, families in America came under direct and fiery attack.

---

[7] K. Gerson and L. Torres, L., *Changing Family Patterns and Family Life. In Emerging Trends in the Social and Behavioral Sciences,* edited by Robert A. Scott and Stephen M. Kosslyn. Hoboken, NJ: Wiley and Sons, 2016.

[8] K. Gerson, *The Unfinished Revolution: Coming of Age in a New Era of Gender, Work, and Family,* New York: Oxford University Press, 2011.

The structure, values, and vision of the family moved from being a single unit that worked together to a collection of individual desires. Many factors attributed to this. There was a rise in the number of mothers who were now employed outside the home. This meant mothers were not home and latchkey kids became the new standard in our communities. Because mom was not home, core values were being taught by secondary sources: neighbors, friends, church and civic programs, electronic platforms — television, radio, and soon computer — or not at all. These factors led to children believing they were the equals of adults, and asserting their independence of thought and action. This "I have a voice movement" was personified by children, teens, and young adults demonstrating their right to speak directly to adults in all situations. Imagine the anger-filled hearts of adults when their standard of "speak only when spoken to" was not only challenged, but ignored! The rights of the children had been established. Earlier generations had dealt with this phenomenon swiftly and decidedly with corporal punishment. This new generation, unfortunately, did not do that. Instead they began to reason with their children as equals. Spanking a child was now viewed with disfavor. This new paradigm birthed current trends, such as: the time-out process, the protection of a child's feelings over their conduct, medication to control children's behavior, different ways of dealing with the dysfunctional family (as a negative), and optional church attendance as a norm. Children today are independent free agents who often intimidate parents through acts of civil disobedience that disrupt every single aspect of the family structure. Children are now birthed into self-fulfilling prophetic words such as hopeless, troubled, lost, bad, hyperactive, menacing, destined for prison, and regretful. It should be noted that the Supreme Court decision that took prayer out of the schools (*Abington School District v. Schempp*, 1963) corresponds perfectly in time with the accounts listed above.

The Health of the Family Is No Longer the Top Priority of Parents

With individualism came a second, more sinister, outcome: the "Me" generation. Parents by definition should have priorities that revolve around the safety, security, and future of every member of their family. This includes, but is not limited to, a home, education, a legacy (career, financial, and spiritual), daily provisions, and the establishment of the family identity (What does your name stand for?) This is only possible when your foundational principles and priorities are aligned to place your family first. Any deviation from this results in work, civic activities, leisure activities, even church work being placed ahead of the family. The family has farmed out their responsibilities and are no longer a cohesive unit. It is not uncommon to see the family heading in multiple directions in the morning, and passing each other, briefly, during different parts of the evening. If this is your experience, please keep reading.

Family Functions Have Been Replaced with Convenience

The greatest manifestation of a changed reality is the use of the dinner table. In our household, the dinner table

was rarely used for a meal. Instead it was used as a place to do homework, assemble projects, sort mail, store overflow stuff, and just remain pretty. What was missing were the hours of conversation, laughter, timeless teachings, sharing of wisdom, life's course corrections and vision mapping, and the passing down of family assets. The family meal, historically, was the one place where children could be molded, families brought closer together, and apparent dysfunction turned into a process of growth. Yes, I understand that some families would rather be bitten by a swarm of bees than share a meal, but most of us can remember historic meals when life became very clear, parents shared from their hearts, children had their "aha moments," and family membership meant something.

Establishing this tradition was important to me, although I am not sure I was always successful. It was, however, commonplace for my daughter's friends to ask to stay for dinner because they did not have this practice in their homes. What happened to this time-honored tradition? Let's follow the line of illogic: you cannot serve what you did not prepare, and you will not prepare a table (or a meal for that matter) if it is not important. For most of us meals are an issue of convenience. We grab something on our way home from work, and eat that something in front of the television or in our rooms. Talking with one another has been replaced with digital devices that provide input from around the globe. Why in the world would I promote the tired, old babblings of my family when I can gain insight from around the world? Alas, we have fallen into an error-filled practice. In falling into this trap, we have removed the very foundation of the transfer of blessings, identity, legacy, vision, and family strength.

Two Worlds That Need to Coexist Better

The spectacle of technological ease and aid is not going to stop any time soon. Those born knowing only a world with technology cannot imagine doing things any other way. Those of us born before the onset of this techno craziness must now adapt to a changed reality. Our world will continue Renrening, Tweeting, Instagramming, Facebooking, Sina Weiboing (China's Twitter), Marco Poloing, or plain old texting. These varied methods of communication are only going to multiply in type and number of users. The test for the challenged is to learn how these platforms may be used to transmit the messages we value. The number of apps are increasing daily that promote the power of conversation and laughter, share the wisdom of the elders, provide healthy course corrections, chart vision mapping, and demonstrate the passing down of family assets. These two worlds will continue to coexist if those who are foreign to technology embrace the new reality, and do not run in fear.

What Are You Eating?

Out of the abundance of the heart the mouth speaks.[9] There is no doubt that whatever is in you will come out. This truth is clearly seen in how a person feels about authority and obedience. If you are filled with disobedience and the questioning of authority, you will rarely support things such as order, discipline, and standard operating procedures. You will be the person who questions not only the reason for a law, rule, or process, but you will probably take it upon yourself to disregard authority because it is not convenient for you too. Your steady diet of disrespect will be obvious in the way you sabotage things in your life. When anyone with premeditation and malice chooses to confront laws, rules, and procedures, they become an agent of discord. Discord attempts to change or remove the law, rule, or procedure in question. When the process of sabotage is joined with ignoring or breaking the current established order, you have the seeds of rebellion. This is the very essence of America's foundation. It will also be our undoing if left unchecked.

---

[9]   See Luke 6:45.

Two Worlds in Conflict

As mentioned above, there exists a conflict between the old guard of law and order and those that lack reverence for them. The inner commitment to obedience is a healthy quality for the development of a citizen who will support and respect others. But what does this obedience look like in the twenty-first century? Our newest generations believe that they uphold this standard of the law, while objecting to what they see as the corruption of acceptable standards and mistreatment of mankind. There is disagreement about what the law should be based upon and how it should work. The person who is led by obedience to authority will serve faithfully; follow the established procedures to bring about change; and understand that without laws, anarchy would reign. This person also understands that sometimes one must question the rationale of a law or standard. This periodic testing of the relevance of order keeps our structure relevant to the times in which we live. No one generation has the answers to all questions. Every generation must take part in this "great discussion" with a mind to find common ground. Thus, all generations may learn from one another. Respect is necessary for this.

Stoke the Fire

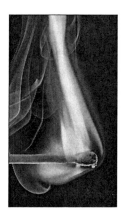

1. We live in a society where failure of character is not only normal, it is to be expected. What do you see as the core reasons that your right has gone so very wrong?

2. We disrespect so many people every single day. What will be your strategy to honor difference in those who are around you?

3. Anger and our inability to move on are often at the core of schisms we have with our fellow man. How does your understanding of authority help you in getting over the knife in your back?

4. We cannot help but say what is overwhelmingly present in our heart. What are you replacing your negatives with, so that your positives are your new confession?

5. Authority, in this age, is ignored. As we speed down the highway, download media without permission, and look for ways to skirt the truth, we are guilty of undermining the line of right and wrong. How are you using the information in this chapter to strengthen your view of right and wrong?

6. Bonus: Convenience has birthed practices and habits that are unhealthy at best, and destructive at worst. What types of habits are you employing that will deliver to you the life you so sincerely desire?

TEST 8

A MEDAL FOR MEDIOCRITY: THERE IS NOTHING COMMON ABOUT YOU!

We live in a "mob-ruled" society. Whatever the majority is persuaded to support or stand for becomes the "correct" position that all are expected to follow. The minority often become not only silent, but forgotten. This is clearly seen in political elections, civic movements, educational norms, and even trends in technology. Thus, if you do not have the tenacity to push through objections and persecution over your choices, your voice may never be heard. It definitely requires courage to move beyond this mediocrity. Where is this island of excellence in the sea of mediocrity? How do we find it? Who is willing to give everything they have to find it?

The Enemy Called Average

The national best-selling author, John L. Mason, with whom I share a similar name, wrote *The Enemy Called Average*.[10] 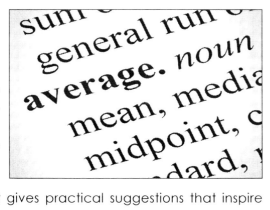 This influential text gives practical suggestions that inspire people to become all that God intends for them, instead of

---

[10] John L. Mason, *The Enemy Called Average*, Bangalore, India: Insight Publishing Group, 2013.

settling for becoming the copies that the world wants. Wow! Mr. Mason was right on target with his title and his assessment. People are driven to morph themselves into a carbon copy of whatever is in fashion at the time. At the writing of this text being "in" means: carrying at least two "smart" devices; understanding how to tweet, chat, surf, tag, and trend; being comfortable with not knowing the purpose of a morning newspaper; believing that all coffee comes in a paper cup through a little window at a drive-through; not understanding why old people get so upset when manners are exchanged for expediency; and finally, believing that a building filled with dusty books in which people went to educate themselves is an urban legend. Laughably, this list is far too short! The enemy called "average" has taken on so many faces that it is difficult to keep track of what persona the majority is hiding behind today. Mediocrity is, in a word, "easy." You may slip into its embrace without really trying. All it takes is a loss of concentration, a simple lapse in judgment, or an ill-advised chance decision that did not work out, to land someone in the valley of average. There you find yourself drifting along without challenge and direction, just going with the flow. The penalty for landing in the sea of mediocrity is the strenuous task of getting yourself out!

Corporate Standards

To make sure that most people are locked into the sea of mediocrity, corporate standards have been established to force compliance. As we read in the last chapter, there must be a healthy respect for and adherence to rules and authority. This principle is built on the contributing truth that those in positions of authority are responsible for our welfare. They would never knowingly lead us astray, so when we follow those in command without understanding what we are being asked to support, we often find ourselves on the wrong side of the fence. How often do we hear about CEOs of multinational corporations agreeing to deals in the name of the company that are against the very core values of that company? How about those instances when corporations are allowed to do things that prey on the elderly, the poor, the uneducated, and the uninformed just so they can increase their profit margin? That sea of mediocrity just got deeper and bigger! Once in its chilly waters, people become subject to wave after wave of hopelessness. This leaves them with few options, or so they think, and with even less opportunity to move on toward excellence. These corporate standards trickle down into every walk of life. Our communities, schools, culture, and even the fashion industry all promote standards that impact our lives. These lists of dos and don'ts keep people in their assigned places like cogs in the machinery. Will they ever fulfill their destiny? Doubtful, unless they rise above the norm and question why their daily diet includes settling for what everyone else is doing.

The Road Less Traveled

To summon the courage to move against the majority, to go against the grain, to be singled out as an independent thinker, to live counterculture, will cost you. Those who choose to stand for what they think is right, even when it is unpopular, run the risk of being persecuted. This is painful. As a result, many people silently follow the majority to avoid this stress. Those with the fortitude to stand against what they believe is wrong, no matter what the consequences, are a rare breed indeed. Greatly blessed are those of us who have a host of these examples in our lives!

Internal Combustion (Motivation)

What causes one person to follow the well-traveled highway with the masses while another takes the path overgrown with shrubs and weeds? Each of us is motivated by different factors. Some are outraged by the unfair treatment of man. Their engine is kicked up a notch every time they see someone mistreated or abused because of their ethnicity, age, class, education, gender, or beliefs. Others are champions for those with lesser opportunities because of their lack of wealth or position. Still others are on a mission to right the wrongs in our society that have been established for a long time. Whatever fuel charges your engine, it is my heartfelt prayer that you find it in abundance of fuel to move you out of the sea of mediocrity. This test cannot be passed without understanding that you, and you alone, are the catalyst for changing your position. If you are moved by an injustice, it is because you were created to bring change to that area. Be courageous and stand against the current to bring that change.

Standing by Yourself or Playing without the Ball

The quest for excellence in all we do, think, say, or represent is a solitary and often lonely journey. We cannot count on the masses to encourage us, and we cannot look to a plethora of examples to see how this path should be conquered. We are often left to our own imagination, our inner voice, and the guiding hand of the Lord above. Armed with only an inner conviction that must show itself strong and agile, we move forward. On our own, the influence and attraction of the mediocre multitude is nowhere in sight. We see the occasional traveler on this isolated road, and we enjoy his company for a season. But that is all. We do not rely on the "ball" to encourage our play. In fact, we often find that the "ball" gets in our way. What we need is the light of inspiration, the knowledge that what is excellent to us is firmly established within us, and a made-up mind that we will see this to its end.

The enemy called "average" relies upon the unwillingness of the masses to find themselves, and move to the next level. Instead they choose to swim in that sea of mediocrity. It feels so right. It agrees with everyone else. It does not make waves. The mediocre requires mindless (or at least misguided) masses to uphold their agenda and move their mission forward. Meanwhile, the minority waits silently for an opportunity to demonstrate that they have a valid opinion. That they are standing on sacred ground where excellence and truth reside. Excellence is essential to the stability of character. Without knowing who you are, what you stand for, and what you were placed on this planet to accomplish, you will forever be influenced by the sirens' song of the wonders of mediocrity. This is why "average" is the enemy. Agreeing with its agenda keeps us from fulfilling our own purpose. Instead we waste our lives, and our lives are precious.

Stoke the Fire

1. The very essence of this book was brought home in comparing myself to John L. Mason (the other one). What are you doing to ensure that your life is not tied to a level of mediocrity?

2. It is really hard to move against the majority in the minds of many people. What are your key motivators that move you in the direction of your purpose, and not backward to the comfort of your stagnant place?

3. It is time to question if you are really operating to your fullest level. What does your "best" look like? How will you get there?

4. Children know how to play by themselves; they do not need others for enjoyment. What are you doing to challenge the assumption that you have no more to give?

5. The world will teach you that being mediocre is easy. You don't have to give your best, just don't be the worst in the bunch. The world is waiting for what is in your being. What will you do to unlock the true potential in you that the world is waiting for?

6. Bonus: Excellence is necessary. What will you do tomorrow to ensure that excellence is the standard and norm, not the exception?

TEST 9

LIVING LIFE ON PURPOSE: BREAKING AND BRIDLING THE "BEAST" WITHIN

We are in the fight of our lives. We strive for lives that are worthy of emulating the Lord and Savior Jesus Christ, while attempting to conquer the twofold nature of our being. We have a higher nature that understands and strives for excellence. We also have a lower nature that is crass, base, and wishes to return to our hunter/gatherer beginnings. In the jungle things were so much simpler! Kill, cook, eat, sleep, repeat. That still resides deep in our DNA, and peeks its curious head above the surface of our consciousness at the most regrettable times! We are trying our best to keep the "beast" in chains. But why? These primal instincts and habits have evolved, as have we, into modern day pursuits and ambitions. Hunting has morphed into the pursuit of careers or accomplishments. Conquest is still the same, but people have been replaced by projects, status, and mobility. The challenge is to train the "beast" to be our servant, and not our undoing — to allow these instincts to drive us to noble pursuits and higher callings. The beast unchecked has ruined, demoralized, and unhinged many, many a valiant warrior.

When I Grow Up

The goal is to grow up and put away old ways of doing things. This includes childish behaviors. Playfulness, coarse

speech, unbridled anger, insatiable thirst for conquest, and lack of character are but a few of these juvenile attributes. People grow into respectful citizens who are governed by acts of faith, honor, chivalry, selflessness, love, and respect. Their character should speak so loudly that their words are unnecessary. Yet most people today are having a hard time with this balancing act. Fosdick stated, "Most folk are in one of these two classes: barbarians with penitent and wistful interludes, or good men with unconquered mutinies." This Dr. Jekyll and Mr. Hyde tension lives in every one of us, governed only by our humility and submission to the Lord that created the "beast" in the first place. As covered in other chapters, our current generations are far too preoccupied with "stuff" to remember that the only way to gain ground on this inner battle is through long-term teachable moments, from the time we are children through our adult years. Adults who have missed countless opportunities to learn life lessons in "beast management" are often trapped and enslaved to the very core principles that, if tempered, would make them successful in any field. Thus, growing up is not nearly as important as having mentors, role models, and positive environments *when* you grow up. The good news is that it is never too late to begin the process of growing up.

Maturity Comes with a Price

When we are young, we cannot wait to grow up and do the things that were forbidden in our youth. Smoking, drinking, going to parties, and exercising freedom are the daydreams of many of our youth. How did their view of adulthood and maturity get so unbalanced? We teach our children that the only good "beast" is a dead "beast"! To accomplish this, we try to modify a child's behavior as he grows. The trouble is we are focused on appearances, and not their hearts. A playful child who seems to have a problem keeping still is "handled" until such time that he learns the dos and don'ts of acceptable behavior. Very rarely is this child challenged to harness his inner desires, and use them to explore his dreams and passions. This is the road to finding and fulfilling destiny. The repressed child never understands the balance required to attain the purpose locked inside him. How sad is the frequent admission that "I don't know my purpose" or "Why can't I reach my purpose, no matter how hard I try?" It does take a village to raise a child, and without an understanding of balance, the child pays the price and grows into a troubled adult.

We Fight What We Cannot Control

Back to our Dr. Jekyll and Mr. Hyde example. It is no wonder that some of us are perceived as angry, out of control, distant, and troubled. If we are fighting the part of ourselves that we cannot control, there is a civil war in progress on most days. We strive to keep the chains on our "beast," never having been taught the secrets of balance. We attend every seminar, read every self-help book, and invest in every new gizmo that will provide insight into our deficiencies. We end up well-read, slightly amused, but unbridled still in our lives. This fight is the surest sign that a person is having balance and control issues in his life. Spot someone who is prone to flying off the handle, impatient over the natural development of others, or just plain lost and I will show you someone whose "beast" is at the wheel of their lives. Scary picture, huh? An unmanageable "beast" trying to change gears! We must make a concerted effort to learn the lessons we missed growing up. Here are a few:

- Unconditional love trumps all.
- Play nice in the sandbox—Collaboration is always more effective than isolation.
- There is more than one way to do most things. Stop being overbearing!

- The greatest thing most of us will remember is a true friend.
- Your legacy must be planned before it is built.
- Remember that there is no place like home.
- Allow your ambition to support another's purpose. Celebrate *someone else's* gifts!
- If it feels wrong, it probably is!
- Take time to play. All work and no play...
- Everyone is better after a nap.

Disqualification and Progress

In order to move forward with our lives, we must first accept disqualification from the "beast" mode. There is no room for unbridled passions to run amuck in our lives. Our "beast" must be broken and bridled for us to progress into our destiny and purpose. This humbled flesh contains our core motivation and drive. These ancient instincts and passions are God's fuel for our spiritual jetpacks. When you realize you need real balance to attain your spiritual stride, you will bring yourself into submission so you can reach your potential. It is the only way.

The test of breaking and managing our inner beast is the only key to unlock our deepest dreams, plans, giftings, and destiny. This spiritual fuel is waiting for our careful assignment to its rightful place. Fosdick wrote,

> "In a slum neighborhood a boy is born magnificently endowed with the old native instincts— ambition, pugnacity, adventurousness, self-regard. In the slums, however, they find

few natural channels to flow in where they will
do anybody any good. They find perverse and
primitive expression. They may land their owner
in Sing-Sing [prison] or the death chair."

What Fosdick understood is that without the accompa-
nying social context for these ancient instincts a person may
still go astray. This is where the church comes into play. The
modern church should provide the necessary shelter in which
a person may break and bridle their beast, and receive instruction in putting their baser parts to work on building their destiny.
Many a writer has made mention of the way a simple piece of
coal is turned into a magnificent diamond. We cannot afford
to overlook a single piece of coal, believing it is only good for
our outdoor grill. These "diamonds in the rough" are the key to
transforming the society we complain about daily.

Stoke the Fire

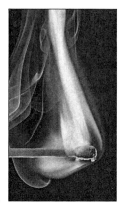

1.   Time, pressure, and a lump of coal are all that is necessary to form a precious stone. What will it take for you to see the people around you in the same fashion?

2.   The beast of our unbridled nature must die. List five things that you will do to move away from your self-absorbed motivations to a higher form of functioning.

3.   I have heard it said many times, "He is just a big kid!" List the things in your life that you can admit are childish. Now, what will you do to rid yourself of these things?

4.   We struggle against our base nature each and every day. Now that you are equipped with some new tools, what will you do to keep your base nature in its rightful place?

5.   Balance is required to make this complex puzzle complete. What is your strategy to bring your life into a new sense of balance?

6.   Bonus: Much of our world does not know how to play any longer. What great lessons have you "lost" since you decided to "grow up"?

TEST 10

A MERCIFUL HEART: CARING FOR OTHERS MORE THAN YOURSELF

Mankind has learned, much to our shame, how to hold and maintain a grudge. We see this in the art of the feud. Feuds are nothing more than unforgiveness giving way to a grudge, and birthing an action against another. Simply put: the person who will not forgive has given themselves over to the greatest depth of egotism. How? Selflessness is the act of *always* preferring another over yourself, so choosing not to forgive is the art of *always* preferring yourself instead. It is the opposite of God's design.

This test traces our ability to maintain a merciful heart: that place where you actively seek to bless those who curse you. In the last chapter, we spoke about breaking and bridling the beast that rests within us. This is the logical next step: to allow our fellow man off the hook, to show mercy. Love will cover the person who misses the mark. Love will also cover the person who is offended by the mistake that was made. To restore our brother or sister requires us to first forgive, and then put love into action. The person who masters this principle will find few people who can remain their enemies.

The Art of Brokenness

We use the term "broken-ness" primarily to describe the result of someone hurting us. A second use of the word is the

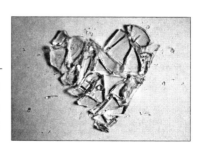

state of being after we have taken our selfish desires, our ego-tism, and our self-righteousness and place them in the hands of the loving God we serve. We place them in *His* hands because we know that only through *His* help can we change. This sec-ondary state is where we feel the hurt of others, hear their tears hitting the pillows in the night season, and know that there is only a small distance between them and us. Brokenness is not a single act, but way of living to which we commit ourselves daily. We wake up, committing ourselves to forgive and show mercy, letting go of those things that would bind us up.

Not Judging, but Showing Mercy

I find myself constantly evaluating others' situa-tions, products, children, work ethic, and a thousand other points that are none of my business. I find myself seeking others who share in these evaluations, and with whom I can communicate my feel-ings. I find myself strengthened by the knowledge that others have now validated what I knew to be true all along! I find myself now planning on how I will confront the unsuspecting person to tell them this validated "truth" and what I think they should do to "fix it." I find myself prostrate on the floor, begging God to forgive me for sitting in this judgment seat, void of His forgiveness and mercy. Then I find myself going back to the process of breaking my inner beast further because my pre-vious actions tell me he is still alive. I find myself forgiving "me" first, and allowing God's love to move me beyond judgment into the practice of showing mercy. In the end, I breathe easier as I recognize that this will always be a continual process and that I am growing in Christ as I walk in mercy.

Allowing No Room for Bitterness

My mother was a master gardener. She got up long before it was hot, and began her work for the day. This included pruning, weeding, digging, edging, watering, and planting. It also included the discernment to know

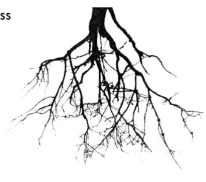

how deep a root was on something she was pulling up. She simply pulled some of them up, but she had to dig around others before the root would give way. How did she know the difference between the two? She had dealt with them long enough to know the difference. This is simple wisdom. Through her experience my mother had learned what she was dealing with: We must all learn to do this. When we remember that our goal is to treat every issue as God would, there is simply no room for allowing the selfishness of unforgiveness. When we hold on to unforgiveness, we become bitter over time. You can always tell someone who has borne the fruit of bitterness, for there is no joy in their being. They will find fault, problems, and a reason to condemn every person they meet. They are just grouchy people!

I have often told the Bible story of the three Hebrew boys who were thrown into the furnace by a wicked king. The miracle was they emerged from the furnace completely unhurt and not even smelling like smoke! If you have gone through an ordeal in which your very being was tested, yet you emerge without lasting damage, you often claim victory. There is another step I want you to take, however. Check to see if you smell like smoke. The lingering effects of smoke are well known. It gets into everything! If you have survived a fire in your home, you know too well how the smoke was the real issue, not the fire. Walls, furniture, books, dishes, every surface was touched by the smoke. The same is true when we are tried by fire in our lives. The fire produces smoke that goes far beyond the actual flames, and attempts to rest on things we don't even imagine.

WARNING! *This next portion may step on your toes a bit!* The person who has been hurt in a relationship in which a covenant was broken may survive the breaking from the other person, but they may still carry the smoke of the betrayal. This smoke rests on their thinking, their actions, their level of trust, their friends, their view of life, and their ability to love. When the next relationship presents itself, the first whiff of smoke-laden garments may send love running for the hills. There is nothing wrong with that person except that healing has not penetrated to the smoke level.

Smoke removal and root removal have the same process. You must first isolate the intended area of removal, and then allow the strong grip of the Spirit of God to penetrate the area. Only then will the root (or the smoke) give way. The root may attempt to grow back. Just keep repeating the process as often as is necessary. There may be an area in your life that was once covered, but when exposed is saturated by smoke. Again, repeat the process as necessary. God is never tired of assisting us. His mercy endures forever.

Pressure Bursts Pipes

The pressure that our daily lives places upon us is not always seen immediately. For some it takes time and even an inspection before they realize that their infrastructure has been compromised. I returned home this week from a business trip to see water in my driveway. This is not generally an issue, as there are parts of my driveway where water pools after it rains, and it had rained earlier that day. When I parked my car, I began to inspect the water and found it was in the wrong place. This led to further inspection, and the discovery that there was a dripping coming from the ceiling of my garage. This observation led to greater concern.

The presence of water from my ceiling was a clear indication that water was flowing somewhere it had no business being. The pipes that were designed to move the water from one place to another were not functioning properly. I immediately went to the upstairs bathroom and looked at possible sources. There it was! A pooling of water at the base of the commode. Turning off the master valve stopped the water, but the pipes had been compromised. This meant that the commode was not functioning, and needed to be repaired or replaced.

Our lives are filled with piping, moving things from one area to another. When pressure has burst these pipes, this process will not work. It must be repaired. Although duct tape has become the solution for a host of problems, a compromised infrastructure will only be repaired by a permanent fix. Take a moment and inspect your personal pipes. Do they show signs of wear and tear? Do they move things as efficiently as they once did? Perhaps it is time for you to open the walls of your heart and allow for a permanent fix.

Dealing with Your Inner Demons

There is no limit to the ways your mind will play tricks on you. Many of us are in bondage to ghosts of our past. We have moved past the initial issue, but are still chained to it in our mind. When we pass a certain location, smell a certain fragrance, see a certain car, eat a certain food, deal with a certain subject, or even think certain thoughts, we are immediately transported to the scene of the crime. Whatever was done to us still has us in bondage. You say, "I have forgiven that person!" That is excellent, but have you forgiven yourself? Have you given yourself permission to move forward? Have you asked the Father to remove these thoughts from your mind? Have you replaced these thoughts with others that are in line with being whole? This is another instance of seeing "smoke" in the strangest places.

To attain the level of Jesus in befriending everyone we meet (and those we have not met yet), forgiving those who may have wronged us, and unconditionally loving others is a lifelong goal. This test will only be a reality as we challenge ourselves to move beyond what we want to what Christ wants. We must follow His example in every area of our lives.

Stoke the Fire

1. We are just now learning the results of pressure on our lives and body. Based on this chapter, what will you look for in your life that may be compromised?

2. Ebenezer Scrooge made dealing with the ghosts of our past commonplace. Looking back on your past, have you successfully removed the negative reminders of your "could have" and "should have" life?

3. If we live long enough we will see that bitterness (internal) has many unintended consequences. What triggers can you name that are still present as a result of not fully forgiving people in your past?

4. Many have seen our ego, soul, and personality (and the selfishness that rests within it) likened to a diamond. What will it take for you to smash that cubic zirconia into a million pieces?

5. One of the James Bond movies is called *Live and Let Die*. We LOVE to make sure that the other person is worse off than we are. What steps are now underway in your life to develop mercy as a new operational strategy?

6. Bonus: List five habits you will develop to help those who cannot help themselves?

TEST 11

STONES OF REMEMBRANCE: HONORING AND BUILDING ON YOUR HERITAGE

God instructed the children of Israel to place stones as a memorial for an event. This was done so that anyone who passed that location would remember the Lord their God and what *He* did. The Israelites were not defined by these past events, but their future was built upon it. A true test of character is whether or not a person has integrated his heritage into present existence and future plans. It has been said that we are the sum total of our DNA's experiences. This would mean that we are the collected vision of all who have gone before us. Once upon a time our heritage was a source of great pride, inspiration, and strength. As our society has grown away from a Christian worldview and simultaneously become more digitally influenced, we are seeing segments of the younger generations believing that they are *self-made* individuals. They seem to think their very existence transcended all that came before them. The loss of our cultural heritage has made orphans of many who have no idea who "their people" are. They see the stones and they note the landmarks, but these structures have no significance to them. This "forgetting" is a great loss because unless you know where you came from, it is very difficult to find the place you are going.

Where Do You Come From?

Family reunions used to be so much fun for me. They were a chance to get together with family members I had not seen in a very long time. As I grew older, however, life got in the way of these opportunities to connect with my people. It seemed that we only got together when someone passed on. This was a sad reason for a family reunion. Yes, the family was together, but it was a time of heavy and burdened hearts, not the joy that reunions brought. These gatherings did not include games and laughter. In my last visits to my extended family I saw cousins for whom learning "who was who" was not the least bit important. In fact, the introduction of family members seemed to be a burden for them. What happened to our family traditions? What happened to the strength of our heritage? People had forgotten where they came from. The loss of this knowledge came at a very great price: we had lost the foundation of our past. In my family that meant losing the stories of landowners and farmers, founding members of the Union of Sleeping Car Porters, Ford certified mechanics, colored schoolteachers (when schools were not integrated), executives, and the list goes on! What a loss! The result of this kind of disconnect is hard to even think about. We had lost their stories. Our stories!

Who Has Impacted You?

We value the things that have had an impact on our lives. If our heritage has never been impressed upon us, it is not surprising that this area seems unimportant to us. Wouldn't it be great if your family exposure went far beyond your immediate family? The world-renowned educator Henry Louis Gates Jr. introduced the world to a scientific process for determining where your ancestry began. Many an inquisitive person has traced their family tree to the Middle East, West Africa, Native American Indian, and Europe. Websites such as ancestry.com allow people to dig into their past. All of these efforts are to provide information that clarifies who you really are. We are indeed the sum total of all who have gone before us.

This application goes deeper than those who came before us though. There are others who are not blood relatives, but still part of our heritage because they have spoken into our lives. They have gone out of their way to ensure that we were taken care of, looked after, provided for, and protected. They demonstrated what love looked like. They took the time to coach, teach, train, and mentor us in a thousand different ways. They were the examples on which we patterned our lives. Some of these extended family members have been with us for decades, and others for just a few years. Either way they have impacted our lives in such a forceful way that our very existence has been transformed. They hold a special, and significant, place in our hearts and history.

Our Scars Birthing Our Stories

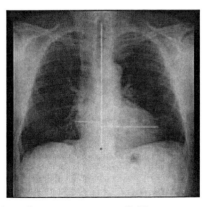

We all have physical scars that are the result of the trials of our lives. Some are barely visible to the casual observer, while others remind us of the goodness of God, and how His hand of protection brought us through. We have emotional and maturation scars as well. These are invisible to anyone who was not with us during the actions that caused them. Yet it is these scars that connect us with our brothers and sisters in Christ in a very real way. There is no greater bond than the one forged when people go through similar trials and tribulations, and emerge victoriously together. There is power in the unity of the body of Christ. When a corporate body understands this, we are no longer ashamed of what we have gone through. Instead we use these scars as stones of victory, praise, and overcoming. For each scar we have, there is a time that God showed Himself strong on our behalf. We praise Him first for delivering us, and then for allowing us to be a vehicle in delivering others.

Stones of Remembrance

The West African tra-
dition of the griot still exists
today. The griot was the
storyteller of a village—the
person who kept the group's
knowledge fresh, under-
stood the power of the heritage of a people, and the
vehicle through which that
heritage found a voice. The
griots used the talking drum,
communal fires, and their
imagination to match stories
with the people. They used their gifts to make sure the people stayed tied together. The families also did their part. They set aside time for the griots to do their work. They could have easily said, "I'm sorry but it has been such a long day. Maybe next time…" Our society has microwaved family time into obscurity. First we compromised the family dinner hour into the family eat-in-front-of-the-television habit. This did two things: It made nightly dinner casual and often insignificant, and second, it reduced the art of conversation by establishing the television

as the focal point of the meal instead of the family itself. We have also made portable communication devices indispensable as an "every second of every minute of every hour of every day" attachment to our bodies. This meant that texting, tweeting, calling, posting, surfing, pinning, and basically being distracted constantly became commonplace in our lives. Very rarely do you see two people having a meal without the presence of some device. Family time is on a life support system. It's no wonder that we have not been successful at presenting the stones of remembrance and their essential messages of the goodness of God to our families. The celebrated and hallowed ground where we met God every day is now crowded by the idols of convenience and technology.

This test requires the active, continuous, and often unpopular stance that we will not be moved from certain family traditions. We will have dinner as a family, and your devices are not invited. We will have a time to talk as a family, and your constant friends, the television and the computer, are not invited. We will rehearse the stories of our heritage, and it doesn't matter if you have heard them once, or a thousand times: You will listen. You will understand that the griot tradition is alive and well, and vital to the success of our families, collectively and individually. These practices are more vital to our health than we even realize.

My Gray Hair

Lack of magnesium, my foot! When I was not the keeper of the stories generated by my branch of the Mason clan, my head was jet black. I didn't worry about why things were so important, why they had to be taught to our children, and why our very identity rested upon the successful completion of this task. Now, a half a century in the making, my understanding is beginning to mature. The stones of remembrance that line the path upon which I walk serve as a constant reminder of the goodness of God, His hand of provision and care, and His unfailing love and faithfulness to His children. When we accepted Him as our Father, His Son as our Lord and Savior, and His indwelling Spirit as our guide, we adopted a new way of looking at life. These stones are not just trinkets strewn as a monument to something that was significant a hundred years ago. These stones are a constant reminder of the love and protection that God wraps us in daily. It is this daily provision that sustains us in the times that are difficult. We are never alone. There is always hope. There is never a lack that will not give way. He is always standing ready to show Himself strong on your behalf.

The oldest stone in my arsenal is a family Bible that is carefully kept in a zip-top bag. Its contents are so fragile that to handle it means possible disintegration. Yet its very existence is a reminder that I have DNA coursing through my veins that dates back as far as we can find records of believers in Jesus Christ. This is not a new trend, but a heritage that I proudly embrace. My gray hair is well worth the responsibility it reflects.

Stoke the Fire

1. We live in a generation that values very little of our past. They are pressing toward the newest, bigger, more improved, and technologically superior way of doing things. What are your favorite memories that have put a smile on your face in the midst of troubling and hard times?

2. Many homes are filled with heirlooms, handed-down treasures from generations long past. Imagine several of these treasures. Why do these items have value far beyond money to you?

3. Christmas remains my favorite holiday. It is purely because of the many family traditions that occur during this season. What is your favorite family tradition? What makes this particular tradition so special to you?

4. Our lives are filled with scars, and shrapnel imbedded deeply within our psyche. Visualize the many scars in your life, and reflect upon the stories associated with each scar. What is the power that these stories hold for you?

5. Most families have a keeper of the records, traditions, history, and experiences gathered over time. This biblically inspired position (Joel 1:3) requires someone who values stories, artifacts, and other items. Who are the keepers of the history in your family? How do these people help in keeping your history alive? How can you help them?

6. Bonus: We are often tied to individuals who are our "brothers from another mother." What binds you to other individuals who share experiences with you?

TEST 12

NOT UNTIL THE FAT LADY SINGS: SEEING THINGS TO THE END

Arlena Patrice Stinson Mason, my mother, loved everything about the opera. An acclaimed, classically trained soprano who graduated with honors from Central State University, Mrs. Mason could listen to any opera, in any language, and appreciate its lyric majesty. My mother knew more operatic pieces than I could count, and sang them in their original language when no one was looking. One day I asked her, "What does it mean when someone says, 'It ain't over until the fat lady sings?'" She asked, "Where did you hear that?" I told her I'd heard it when I was watching Bugs Bunny. She laughed, and explained to me that in one of the longest series of operas from Richard Wagner's "Ring Cycle," the opera was not over until the main character sang. This was usually a plump singer playing the character of Brünnhilde. This saying has been used ever since to encourage us to persevere until the end because you never knew what might happen.

This last test—perseverance and tenacity—must be mastered if we are to outlast fiery trials. We are faced with the fact that when life gets hard we may give up. Fosdick captured this picturesquely when he painted this picture:

> "Interesting statistics have been compiled by insurance actuaries with reference to the prospects of a hundred average young men twenty-five years of age starting out in business. The results are decidedly disconcerting. Forty

years afterward, when those young men are sixty-five years old, they will on the average have fallen into the following classes: thirty-six dead, fifty-four financially dependent on family or charity, five barely able to make their own living, four well-to-do, one rich. If we discount the unfairness and ill fortune of external circumstance which doubtless are involved in this lame finish of many good beginnings, we still have left a large amount of inability to see life through which must be due to lack of character."

Truly, good beginnings do not guarantee positive, or profitable endings. The end of a thing may be lame. The principle that stands between success and failure is the developed character of the individual.

We have now covered twelve tests that a person will face, and in so doing, have uncovered many principles and practices that will strengthen the individual. This last area may be the most strenuous of all. The dedication of a long-distance runner requires, and in fact, demands that the person push through the parts of the journey in which they would understandably give up. What in the world would make us press forward to the end? What could possibly be so beneficial that personal sacrifice and loss pales by comparison to the accomplishment yet to come?

Are We There Yet?

No adult has escaped this question from a child, a sibling, or just a misinformed passenger. This question is the result of a misconception between

the person asking and the reality of the length of the trip. It doesn't matter if we are going to the corner grocery store or across the country; if the person asking is unaware of the length of the journey, they will ask this question. The same is true when we do a self-assessment of our life's goals and plans. We often ask: "Why aren't we there yet?" This is a juvenile question, given the fact that we have not yet invested the time and effort necessary to reach our goals. If we have not established our pillars of priority, and coupled those to the clear path of a plan, we may never know that our dream cannot become a reality. "Are we there?" becomes a habitual comment, uttered as if progress is being made when it really is not. The truth of the matter is that few people are making progress toward an acceptable end; the remainder are just "lame" according to Fosdick. Many a life coach has observed that at the center of people's lack of drive is a lack of tenacity. They are prone to give up, because they were never trained to improvise, overcome, and adapt. They do not know how to keep at it when times get tough without giving up. Theirs is a world where pain rules their actions. If it costs them more than they are willing to give, they will stop before they start. It is highly discouraging when you are partnered with someone who has no intention of seeing your project to the end. He has already decided which exit he will take to get away from this thing! How did we get so far from a successful process? We give up long before the product we wish to see could ever come forth.

Not What I Expected

For many who were intent on changing the world, their perspective of the task was wrong from the start. They believed that getting a college degree could be done without reading or writing papers. They believed that advancing in the company could be done without having to work past 4:00 p.m. They believed that they could raise children on the same budget that they had as newlyweds. They believed that they could make a life-altering splash in the marketplace without personal investment. They believed that there was no connection between their desired outcome and their effort. When they finally woke up to the reality of how much hard work, sweat, and self-sacrifice the job would require, they exclaimed, "This is not what I expected! I don't know if I can do this!" They had deluded themselves, thinking getting to their goal would be a leisurely stroll through the park. We must clearly assess what is required to reach a stated goal, or we deceive ourselves. If we clearly understand the resources we need to accomplish our mission, but ignore these facts because they conflict with our desires, that is also delusional. When we understand what we must do to reach that goal and take an easier path instead, we are on the wrong path and we will not succeed. Planning demands an accurate, thorough, and visionary assessment of the resources, timing, and effort required. Only then can you provide a strategic plan that will birth a project schedule that will meet the mark. Anything short of this will deliver an outline that will change as your goals change. If your goals change like this, you will never accomplish what you first set out to do.

We cannot expect the unexpected, in most cases. What we can do is make contingency plans for those things we know will occur along our path. If our goal is to sell handbags in New York, it is clear that a retail space, online presence, or other delivery method is essential for our success. These require resources to not only acquire the space, but maintain it too. As simple as this example is, its message is clear: Poor Planning Will Lead to Poor Results. We should be motivated to complete plans that are complex enough to change with an ever-progressing world, but simple enough to explain to our children. Our plans should forever be in front of us, guiding us, leading us, and allowing us to use them as both map and compass.

What Are You Willing to Pay for Success?

The ant doesn't need an introduction. This is one of God's most amazing examples of hard work. The ant is born with tenacity. If it is confronted with an obstacle, it goes over, under, around, or just moves it. You do not have to motivate ants. They are constantly fulfilling their strategic plan by accomplishing predetermined goals and objectives. They send search or scout parties out to find sources of food, while other teams are expanding and building the birthing chambers, and yet another squad is tending to the queen. This symphony of activity is carefully led by internal motivators that have no "off" switch. They are tenacious to the 100th power! This is why homeowners despise them. It is a constant war to keep the ever-charging, never-relenting, always advancing army out of our homes. What a great example they provide as we study this test. If we only learned the lessons that ants are teaching! I mean, really get down to the core principles that they exhibit, and then set ourselves to coach, train, and mentor ourselves and others in mastering these principles. Let's see what that would look like.

1. **Ants are driven by a well-defined purpose.** There is no confusion as to which ant is doing what task. In fact, their dedication to the task that they were born to accomplish is literally encoded in their DNA. The same is true of humans, but we have the option to "choose" if we are going to follow our internal encoding. What would our world look like if we just said "yes" to the plans and visions within us?

2. **Ants communicate even when things are going well.** In the ant world they do not wait until there is a crisis to communicate with each other. Using pheromone triggers the ant can instantly communicate with other ants. We possess this same ability. Our ability to communicate with others is not our problem. Our issue rests in communicating. Constant communication is a rarity in our families, our churches, our jobs, or with friends. We wait until something goes wrong, and then we use every possible avenue of communication to send a distress signal. How efficient it would be if we communicated our successes as well as our trials.

3. **Ants work and think as a team.** Everyone stays in their lane. They have assigned areas of expertise, and are not driven by egotism and power. The result is that excellence in the task they are assigned is the most important thing they can do. There is no ladder for them to climb, so overlooking their assigned task for another assignment is a foreign concept to them. Collaboration is the only language they speak. They know that alone they can accomplish very little, but together there is no limit to what they can do.

4. **Ants set deadlines, and adhere to the established schedule.** This is not funny, but I've often heard that some people would be late to their own funeral! Punctuality is not a pressing issue for some because they do not see the importance of their presence. The ants understand that without deadlines they will face a winter season without all that they need and in which they can no longer work. Therefore in the spring, summer, and fall, they prepare for a time when they can do very little. This is wisdom. They understand the consequences of failing to meet their deadlines, both individually and collectively.

5. **Ants trust one another.** Ants do not only demonstrate a world-class work ethic, they also trust each other to accomplish tasks. You don't see micromanagement, isolationism, or the lone ranger syndrome in the ant kingdom. The ants have unwavering trust in each other, and allow their fellow ants to accomplish their assigned task to the exacting standards established. The symphony is not missing a section of the orchestra. Every instrument is present, and all understand the music being played.

6. **Ants demonstrate how important the next generation is to their survival.** The entire colony works toward producing more ants. The queen is the central figure, but so are defenses, the nursery, food supplies, and supply chain details. The next generation is always on the mind of each and every ant. They carry out their duties with focus, diligence, and tirelessness because the next generation is depending on them. We are still trying to understand the next generation. They are more than a catchy title (Gen X, Gen Next, Millennials, etc.); they are breathing and living beings who are curious about their destiny. Are we prepared to provide them with a map showing them where they are to go?

7. **Ants teach us that knowledge must be shared.** What a perfect way to transfer information! Ants leave chemical signals for their comrades to find and take action. The ant instinctively knows that it will be better off with others knowing what it knows. Their vast corporate knowledge is shared at an alarming rate. They understand that only by sharing information and knowledge will the entire colony benefit. Wow! This teaching is the antithesis to the cry of: "I've got mine, you get yours!" This is also contrary to the folks who say, "When you live as long as I have, you may start to learn what I have forgotten." What cruel and useless demonstrations of

our egocentric nature these are. If we moved beyond ourselves for just a short while, we would understand how precious the sharing of knowledge actually is. Imagine a world where the passing on of knowledge was as commonplace as exchanging business cards. Where mentoring was the standard for up-and-coming young people. Where coaching and training was available, not for cost, but for the asking. Imagine a world where we valued the collective knowledge of our communities, and experts scheduled their time to fill in gaps where these communities were lacking. What an amazing possibility this would create!

Putting Your Hand to the Plow

And Jesus said unto him, "No man, having put his hand to the plough, and looking back, is fit for the kingdom of God" (Luke 9:62). My great-grandfather and my grandfather were farmers. They cultivated, sowed into, cared for, and harvested the land. They demonstrated that crops would not miraculously appear just by wishing that you had a head of cabbage or a tomato. Farming is hard work. My grandfather had two regular jobs, but kept his seven-acre garden because it provided for his family. In those days, expenses were decreased by doing things yourself. To a city kid these practices only birthed questions: Why do you put the peanuts on top of the shed roof? Don't you need some salad dressing for that tomato? What do you learn from plucking a watermelon? What does frost do to collard greens? If you can't see the vegetable in the ground, how do you know it is ready to be picked? What does it mean to have a "tough row to hoe"? We did our best to master the skills that my grandfather had learned as a child, and spent his entire life developing. We only had a couple of weeks a year to show a knack for this work. What we demonstrated was that we were children whose food came from the grocery store. The work needed for the land to yield to us was foreign. I really did have a tough row to hoe! The only problem was that I did not even understand what that meant. I was a city dweller. For others like me, the phrase comes from a farming mindset. You often tilled the ground to create the furrows in which you planted seed. The larger your land, the longer the rows; and the more debris that had to be removed (sticks, rocks, roots, hardened clay), the harder the task. When you looked at the row ahead of you, the picture became clear. Fast forward to right now. You are faced with a gargantuan plot of land known as your destiny. You may, or may not, have spent the time cultivating the land to plant good seed. It may be filled with sticks (dead pieces of previous dreams), rocks (obstacles that stand in the way of your dreams), roots (what is left when you cut down unwanted dreams, but forgot to pull up), and hardened clay (a type of soil that must be worked to deliver a return). You put your hand to the plow, and begin your work. So far, so good. At about your fortieth acre, it seems like it will never end, so you sneak a peek at what you have already accomplished. That action causes your plow to go off course, and you have to do the whole row all over again!

The deeper issue is exposed by Jesus in the Gospel narratives. Your distracted tendencies have disqualified you from service in the kingdom. That can't be right! Alas, it is 100 percent true. If you begin a work, only to look backwards (a sign of regret, multiple priorities, or distraction), you cannot have your first goal in your mind anymore. This loss of focus immediately compromises the task. Jesus made this point abundantly clear: "If you are going to follow Me, leave all the rest of your messy life alone." Only by casting off all our cares will we embrace the focus we need to accomplish what God has given us. Our perseverance, tenacity, and desire to reach the end is simply demonstrated by holding our plows straight. Each furrow is the same distance apart, the same length, and the same depth. It may indeed be a hard row to hoe, but when we are focused and looking ahead, we are not persuaded to turn back. We have made up our minds, set our course, counted the cost, and now we are working toward a planned end. We cannot drive the car forward by looking in the rearview mirror without crashing.

Every farmer understands the need to employ basic biblical principles in their work. They grow patient by knowing that seed time and harvest are separated by time and hard work. They understand long suffering by seeing what the seed must go through in order to spring forth with new life. They demonstrate love by forgiving God's children that may illegally take crops that they neither worked to plant nor harvest. It is time for you to establish the needed fruit within your strategic plan to fulfill your destiny. Only by using these basic skills will you also have the correct mental and spiritual posture to endure the storms that will challenge you.

Stoke the Fire

1. Be not weary in well doing. It is a great sentiment, but it's not easy to do in normal life. What do you see as the core motivator to see something to the very end?

2. The work ethic of the ant is often generalized to what mankind should do. What lesson from the ant do you find hardest for you to master? Why?

3. Our patterns in life and work are often passed down from generation to generation. What lessons did you learn from your parents or grandparents? Did you follow the lessons, or did you choose to deviate from that training? How did this impact your life?

4. The cemetery is filled with countless inventions, cures, and world-shaking ideas. What next generation idea is within you? How are you going to believe the reports from your ancestors concerning you?

5. Where are you going with your life? How will you know when it is time for the fat lady to clear her throat?

6. Bonus: This may be the hardest lesson of all! What will it take for you to withstand the obstacles that may come into your life, and maintain the peace and mercy necessary to see your vision through to the end?

FINAL EXAM

In the previous twelve chapters, we have covered some monumental areas within which your character may be challenged. You have been brought to this final place, hopefully, after you have used these pages as a guide to fireproof your life. How did you do? Thankfully, there is not a real-life test at the end of this book. Instead, think of this as a series of what-ifs you can use to see if you have room for growth. Is there a place within your heart that may require attention?

Adjusting Your Vision

Life is not a check-the-box exercise. There will be times when you succeed, and there will be times when you fail. Prepare yourself to adjust your vision, no matter what. If you succeed, adjust your vision further up for the next level. If you fail, then adjust your vision up for where you missed the mark and begin anew. Your character will deepen as you develop it. Take nothing for granted, and leave nothing unchallenged. Your very destiny rests upon your ability to build the infrastructure to support it. This will not happen overnight, and it will not happen without dedicated work. Now is the time to look yourself straight in the eye and make the necessary adjustments to insure success.

One Final Thought

There is nothing cookie-cutter about developing your character. It has taken me half a century to get to this point. Many times I thought it impossible, but over time I developed in these areas, using the same advice and practical applications that I have provided for you. Some areas I mastered quickly, while others are still under construction. The greatest lesson I learned along the way is that nothing can stand in the way of a person who both understands, and is committed to, their destiny and purpose.

Fosdick began his book by stating:

> "The papers (the original articles written for *The Ladies Home Journal*) are an endeavor to stress some fundamental tests of character which our new generation is tempted to forget. With many overhead schemes for the world's salvation, everything rests back on integrity and driving power in personal character. 'You cannot carve rotten wood,' says a Chinese proverb. Nor can you carve decrepit and decayed character into any economic system or scheme of government that will work happiness for men. It is an old emphasis, but it is indispensable, and just now we may well get back to it."

You were created for a purpose. God saw to it that you were filled with plans, ideas, and visionary greatness which will place you forever in the history of our world. Your only obstacle is identifying and completing what already has been birthed in your spirit. I pray that this text has proven beneficial to you as you follow the Master's lead.

Stoke the Fire

1. This book represents a journey you still have the option to take. Have you used this book to construct a plan? If not, why not?

2. Your vision of yourself may motivate or diminish your ultimate attainment of your life's purpose. What has this book given you as strategies to see yourself as "winning" in this journey?

3. This book is designed for those who have both succeeded and failed. Now that you, hopefully, understand that there is life after both failure and success, what is the strategy for your next chapter?

4. This book has referenced your attitude in many different ways and forms. What do you see as the key to changing how you think?

5. In order to see things through the end, you must have a plan, an accountability group, core motivators, and an end goal. How have you put things in order so that you have measures to see if you are moving forward? What does success look like?

Bonus: You are the best book someone else may ever read. What is the new title for this soon-to-be-released bestseller?

JOHN L. MASON, PH. D.
EDUCATOR, TRAINER, COACH, AUTHOR,
AMBASSADOR OF JESUS CHRIST

Dr. John Mason has been creatively leading teams within higher education institutions for over 25 years. This commitment to advancing knowledge, birthed from a true love to see people grow and develop, has produced servant leaders now deployed in a myriad of disciplines. Dr. Mason's passion, fire and energy rest in the work he does "unpacking" the hidden abilities and dreams of those he encounters.

Using time-honored Biblical principles, Mason holds classes, workshops, and one-on-one sessions to coach, train, and mentor men and women who struggle or may have missed the mark due to the trials of life. Failure, at any level or magnitude, is often the best catalyst to explore and cultivate a person's inner strengths.

Dr. Mason's life has focused on the development of all people (young and old). However, there is a special place within his heart for the development of young men. The focus of this effort is to catalyze a man's calling, dreams, gifts, talents, and purpose. Dr. Mason realizes that very few men are called to full-time ministry. Rather, they are called to exercise the power of "salt and light" in the field of their dreams (the place where God has planted them, and where their expertise and educational training will shine). Mentoring men to walk in excellence, producing industry-leading outcomes, and influencing those around them is the "fruit" of Mason's efforts.

The late Rev. Dr. Martin Luther King, Jr. best illustrates Dr. Mason's philosophy through this passage:

Education must enable one to sift and weigh evidence, to discern the true from the false, the real from the unreal, and the fact from the fiction. The function of education therefore is to teach one to think intensively and to think critically. But education, which stops with efficiency, may prove the greatest menace to society. The most dangerous criminal may be the man gifted with reason but no morals. We must remember that intelligence is not enough. Intelligence plus character – that is the true goal of education. The complete education gives one not only power of concentration, but worthy objectives upon which to concentrate.

Dr. Mason has one daughter, Shamin (B.A., M.Ed.), who currently serves as the Diversity and Inclusion Coordinator, within the Diversity and Community Engagement Office of St. Louis University (St. Louis, MO).

Mason is an avid bowler, loves photography, still loves to read books made of paper, and believes sunrises and sunsets are God's signature for those who have the DNA of the tribe of Issachar (I Chronicles 12:32).

Dr. John L. Mason lives in Douglasville, Georgia, a suburb of Atlanta. He serves as a Faculty member for the Educational Leadership Department, of the Tift College of Education at Mercer University.

For Further Information:
Dr. John L. Mason
4414 Mill Water Crossing
Douglasville, GA 30135
404-449-0810
jmason@masononfire.com
www.masononfire.com
@masononfire

IF YOU'RE A FAN OF THIS BOOK, WILL YOU HELP ME SPREAD THE WORD?

There are several ways you can help me get the word out about the message of this book...

- Post a 5-Star review on Amazon, Goodreads and other places that come to mind.
- Write about the book on your Facebook, Twitter, Instagram, Google+, any social media sites you regularly use.
- If you blog, consider referencing the book, or publishing an excerpt from the book with a link back to my website.
- Take a photo of yourself with your copy of the book. Post it on your social media – email me a copy as well!
- Recommend the book to friends – word of mouth is still the more effective form of advertising.
- When you're in a bookstore, ask them if they carry the book. The book is available through all major distributors, so any bookstore that does not have it in stock can easily order it.
- Do you know a journalist or media personality who might be willing to interview me or write an article based on the book? If you will email mail me your contact, I will gladly follow up.
- Purchase additional copies to give away as gifts.

You can order additional copies of the book from my website as well as in bookstores by going to *www.masononfire.com.* Special bulk quantity discounts are available.

SPEAKING SCHEDULE/Contact Information...

If you, or your organization, are interested in using time-honored and tested Biblical principles for classes, workshops, or one-on-one sessions to teach, coach, train, and mentor men and women who struggle or may have missed the mark due to the trials of life, please contact me at*: jmason@masononfire.com.*

4414 Mill Water Crossing
Douglasville, GA 30135
404-449-0810
jmason@masononfire.com
www.masononfire.com
@masononfire

CPSIA information can be obtained
at www.ICGtesting.com
Printed in the USA
FFOW04n1637080218
44943704-45191FF

9 780998 977379